I LOVE YOU

Those three little words can mean vastly different things to different people—including you and your mate.

Drawing on fresh psychological research and real-life experiences of hundreds of loving couples, the authors of the acclaimed NO-FAULT MARRIAGE help you understand—and improve—your love relationships.

Discover your personal love style by answering the fifty questions in the Love Scale Quiz, designed to help lovers, sweethearts, and spouses identify love from a totally new perspective.

Also by Marcia Lasswell and Norman M. Lobsenz
Published by Ballantine Books:

NO-FAULT MARRIAGE

STYLES OF LOVING

Why You Love the Way You Do

———

MARCIA LASSWELL &
NORMAN M. LOBSENZ

BALLANTINE BOOKS • NEW YORK

Grateful acknowledgment is made for permission to quote portions from the following:

Excerpt from *Beloved Infidel* by Sheilah Graham and Gerold Frank. Copyright © 1958 by Sheilah Graham and Gerold Frank. Reprinted by permission of Holt, Rinehart and Winston, Publishers.

Excerpt from letter to F. Scott Fitzgerald from Zelda Fitzgerald. Copyright © 1963 by Frances Scott Fitzgerald Lanahan. Reprinted by permission of Harold Ober Associates, Inc.

Excerpt from *Bring Me a Unicorn* by Anne Morrow Lindbergh. Reprinted by permission of Harcourt Brace Jovanovich, Inc., 1972.

Excerpt from letter to Frédéric Chopin to Delphine Potocka. Reprinted by permission of George Marek.

Library of Congress Catalog Card Number: 78-22338

ISBN 0-345-29228-6

This edition published by arrangement with
Doubleday & Company, Inc.

Manufactured in the United States of America

First Ballantine Books Edition: February 1981

For our children
—Julie, Tom, and Jane—
—George, Jim, and Michael—
May they find love rewarding

CONTENTS

. . . As there are as many minds as there are heads, so there are as many kinds of love as there are hearts.

—Tolstoy, *Anna Karenina*

PREFACE

Every human being is born with a need to be loved. None of us ever outgrows it. We are born, too, with an urge to love, and we never outgrow that either. Throughout our lifetime love is overwhelmingly the most important source of personal happiness, far outranking such other satisfactions as money, status, fame, or knowledge.

Why, then, do so many men and women have so much trouble giving and receiving love?

Until quite recently there have been only a few scattered attempts to search for realistic answers to that question. Other emotions—fear, anger, jealousy—have been carefully studied. But love as a social and psychological phenomenon has been comparatively ignored. One of the earliest attempts seriously to analyze love ran afoul of the guardians of morality. That happened half a century ago, when a professor at a Midwestern university designed a questionnaire to survey his students' ideas about love. When college authorities learned that the study included questions such as, "Did you ever breathe into the ear of a person of the opposite sex in order to arouse their passion?" they fired the professor on grounds of moral turpitude.[1] Current efforts to learn about love occasionally run afoul of the guardians of economy. Only a few years ago Senator William Proxmire attacked a National Science Foundation grant for research on the nature of love as a "waste" of tax money. "Two hundred million Americans want to leave some things a mystery," the senator said, "and right at the top of those things we don't want to know is why a man falls in love with a woman and vice versa."

There are those of us, however, who believe love should not remain entirely a mystery. Indeed, in a culture where man-woman relationships are built upon the flimsy foundation of romanticism, and where love is considered the chief prerequisite for marriage and parenthood, it seems to us that it is vital to know as much as possible about why and how men and women love each other—and why they don't. One of the authors of this book is a marital therapist. Each week, in her practice, she sees troubled clients whose problems stem largely from confusions about what love is, or may be, and about how differently it is expressed. They make such statements as:

• "I guess I love him, but I'm not *in* love with him anymore."
• "I know what love means to me; it certainly doesn't seem to mean that to her."
• "He says words don't matter, that I should know he loves me because he takes care of me. But I won't feel that he loves me until he *tells* me that he does."
• "I love him, and he loves me, but if we weren't married we wouldn't pick each other to spend an evening with."

After hearing remarks like this often enough, one begins to wonder: what do men and women think they mean when they use the word "love"? What concept do they have of it? How would they define it? The word has become like an old coin, so worn away by its indiscriminate passage through hundreds of thousands of hands that we can no longer identify it with any certainty, or clearly tell what value it represents.

This book, and the current research on which it is based, is designed to help men and women—lovers, sweethearts, spouses—identify love from a totally new perspective. In the past it has been customary to analyze love in quantitative terms: How *much* does he love me? How *long* will she care for me? How *intense* are my feelings? We believe it is far more significant and revealing to examine love in qualitative terms: *How* do I love him (or her)? In what ways do I feel loved? In what ways do I express love? Does my pattern of loving mesh or conflict with my partner's style? In these pages we shall define and analyze six basic styles of love and show how each person can discover his or her particular style. That knowledge can help everyone to understand and to improve his or her love relationships.

We need this clearer knowledge of the anatomy of love: how it is formed, how it grows, how it functions. There are those who say love is too personal to be classified, too fragile to withstand such scrutiny. But analysis does not deprive love of its mystery and charm any more than the study of a flower hinders our appreciation of its beauty and fragrance. Any phenomenon that can bring so much joy and sorrow to so many people needs to be better understood. "Love is blind," Shakespeare wrote, "and lovers cannot see the pretty follies that themselves commit." But why let such a state of affairs continue if lovers' eyes can be opened? If anything, love's many splendors would be enhanced. And the unfortunate results of love misinterpreted, misguided, and misused—unhappy love afairs, sterile or hostile marriages, separations and divorces—might well be prevented or at least minimized. Reliable knowledge about any significant aspect of our emotional life helps us to function more meaningfully. There is no reason for love to be an exception.

We are indebted to many people for help and support in the conception and delivery of this book. Specifically, we are grateful for the encouragement we received from Dr. John Alan Lee, whose researches in love stimulated our thinking, and for his generosity in giving us free access to his findings. We are particularly grateful to Dr. Thomas E. Lasswell and Dr. Terry Hatkoff, who permitted us to adapt their Love Scale Questionnaire for use in this book, and who made available to us much of their continuing research on styles of love. Dr. Lasswell was also enormously helpful in making original suggestions and in validating some of the conclusions we drew from the material. Thanks are due as well to the many individuals and couples who talked frankly with us about their ideas of love and the ways in which various love experiences shaped their lives. But whenever case histories or personal anecdotes are used, names and other non-essential details have been changed to protect the privacy of those involved.

1

THE SEARCH FOR LOVE

I do not know what this love may be
That cometh to all, but not to me. . . .
—W. S. Gilbert, *Patience*

Ever since human society reached that point in civilization when personal survival was no longer the overriding daily concern, the search for love has been the prime preoccupation and chief desire of most men and women. A four-thousand-year-old fragment of a clay tablet, unearthed by archaeologists in the ruins of Babylon, bears a message not too unlike the lovelorn lament of a modern torch song or country-rock lyric. "To Bibiya," the cuneiform inscription reads. "I have come to Babylon and saw you not. Oh, I am so sad." At about the same time, give or take a millennium, an Egyptian woman separated from her lover inked this bittersweet sentiment on a shred of papyrus: "I go for a walk and you are with me in every beautiful place, and my hand is in your hand."

Today, more than nine out of every ten Americans say they believe that love is the most important ingredient in any recipe for personal happiness.[1] True, there are some who willingly abandon or reluctantly sacrifice love for other goals: fame, wealth, worldly achievement, or spiritual purity. But virtually every one of us, at some time or other in his life, glories and suffers in the grip of love's emotional upheaval. If we do not have it, we want it. If we have it, we want more of it, or a different version of it, or a different partner with whom to share it. If our love is unrequited, we are miserable. If we have love and then lose it, we seek to recapture it. Even those who admit to never having experienced love at all still accept that it does, indeed, exist. And they, too, hope to find it.

But while we believe in love, we can seldom agree on what love *is*. The rich fabric of language turns threadbare when confronted even with the basic task of differentiating among the various kinds of feelings encompassed in that single word. Adjectives and adverbs must be called into action: puppy love and conjugal love, companionate love and sexual love, parental love and filial love, brotherly love and friendly love, platonic love and romantic love, mature love and immature love. The fact is that by its nature love has never been and cannot be susceptible to a single precise definition. Words are symbols that organize memories and feelings. A word such as "love" represents an enormous, diverse collection of memories of past experiences and the feelings one has built up around them.

As a result philosophers, poets, scientists, and lovers have all defined it according to their own biases. Plato, for example, declared that loving someone was a way of appreciating the essence of beauty and goodness within that person. To the Roman poet Ovid, love meant playful sexual sport. Andreas Capellanus, who in the twelfth century codified the rules of the art of courtly love, defined love as "a certain inborn suffering derived from the sight of or excessive meditation upon the beauty of the opposite sex." To the French courtesan Ninon de Lenclos, impatiently awaiting the embraces of her newest conquest, love was the "divine fury" of physical passion. John Watson, a leading American psychologist at the turn of the twentieth century, defined love as "an innate emotion elicited by cutaneous stimulation of the erogenous zones." (So much for goodness, sport, suffering, or passion!) To Sigmund Freud, however, love was, in effect, just the opposite. While the desire for sexual union is at the core of the emotion, he said, when that desire is blocked one compensates for the disappointment and frustration by idealizing the other person and falling in love with him or her. Still another psychological view of love is offered by Erich Fromm in his classic book, *The Art of Loving*. He identifies love as a device we employ to relieve our sense of emotional isolation. Loneliness, Fromm asserts, is a basic human condition in our culture, and "falling in love" is a way to cope with it.

Social scientists, who have intensely analyzed such harsher aspects of human behavior as aggression, violence, and prejudice, have until recently paid little attention to love. "It is strange," wrote family sociologist William M. Kephart a few years ago, "that in a society in which romantic love presumably serves as the basis for marriage, love itself has been largely rejected as a topic for serious study."[2] This benign neglect of the most significant area of personal relationships is doubtless due, in part, to the difficulty of trying to explore love by traditional sociological methods. As we shall see, most previous attempts to measure or to understand why and how people love each other have been frustrated by difficulties—not the least of which is the general inability of everyone concerned to agree on what they are talking about.

In any event, social scientists tend to sweep love under a rug conveniently labeled "emotional need satisfactions." Under this catchall, loving is thought to be a way of meeting one's needs: to be dominant or dependent, to give or to receive nurturing and emotional support, to shore up a weak ego—one's own or another's—or to compensate for real or imagined inadequacies in one's personality. A few social scientists go so far as to define love as an "addiction," a pathological attachment to a person who becomes one's chief or only source of gratification. In this view, love, like a drug, serves as a way of escape from oneself. The ordinary man and woman have so far paid remarkably little heed to these various attempts to define or analyze love. They are content, it would seem, to accept love for what Victor Herbert described it as— the "sweet mystery of life," a phenomenon one seeks without needing to understand, a state of being which one falls into joyously and out of sadly, and in either case with equal puzzlement.

But here a question arises: Is that a sensible attitude to take toward perhaps the basic factor in human relationships? When a couple marry they promise to love, honor, cherish, respect, support each other. To some extent both persons know, in their minds or hearts, what specific feelings, thoughts, and behaviors are involved in honoring, cherishing, respecting, and supporting. They are far more vague about what they mean by loving. And certainly neither person can be any more certain about what his or her partner means by it. The unsettling fact is that two persons may believe themselves to be very much "in love" with each other yet have quite different ideas of what that means—of what love is, or, more important, how to express it.

For example, it is not uncommon for one partner to

feel quite loving toward the other while at the same time
the other feels unloved. It is as if they are on two different emotional wave lengths. "But you never tell me that
you love me," she may say. "I shouldn't have to tell you.
I do loving things for you," he replies. Those "loving
things" may in his eyes include such actions as bringing
home his pay check, fixing broken appliances, avoiding
arguments. In her eyes they are all merely things any
good man should routinely do. She defines evidence of
love as words of endearment, gifts, touching, tenderness
—the kinds of behavior that *he* is perhaps uncomfortable
with. And yet he knows he loves her. And yet she is not
getting that message. In other words, love is more than
an emotion. Love is also an intellectual concept. Love is
what you *think* it is.

Is it, then, reasonable for lovers to make no serious
effort to try to understand the workings of a stimulus that
can provoke two (and a hundred other) different reactions? It is not really important that everyone agrees on a
single definition of love. What *is* important is to acknowledge that each of us has a definition that is real and vital
to ourselves. Our loving actions are based on that definition just as our partner's actions are based on his or hers.
You may not like, or even understand, other ideas and
ways of loving. But unless you accept a partner's definition,
and unless he or she accepts yours, there is a good chance
that the ways in which each of you expresses love will go
unappreciated or be misinterpreted.

"OF THE PLEASURE THAT PASSION GIVES, I SEE NOTHING"

Most Americans today automatically assume love is a
prerequisite for happy marriage. But that notion is a
historically recent one. In earlier times love, passion, and
romance were usually the forerunners of tragedy; they
seldom if ever were expected to lead to an enduring or
fulfilling relationship. To love, a European nobleman told
his adored one, is to suffer: "I suffer in advance from the
suffering that is to come," he ardently declared. Consider,
for instance, Marianna Alcoforado, a nineteenth-century
Portuguese beauty, and her beloved, a captain in the army
of Napoleon. After their rapturous affair the officer was
recalled to France. Marianna wrote him dozens of burning

letters. He never answered any of them. But the pangs of unrequited passion only served to inflame Marianna's feelings. "I thank you from the bottom of my heart for the despair you cause me," she wrote. "I despise the tranquillity in which I lived before knowing you. Farewell, my passion grows with every moment."

In medieval days, when the concept of courtly love flourished in Europe, men did battle or embarked on hopeless quests for the honor of their ladies. But their ladies were always other men's wives, for it was held that marriage and love had nothing to do with each other. Indeed, *could* not. Noble men and women held "courts of love" at which such questions were seriously considered. One much-quoted judgment handed down by Marie, Countess of Champagne, summed up many similar findings: "We hold that love cannot exert its power between two people who are married to each other. For lovers give each other everything freely, under no compulsion of necessity; but married people are in duty bound to give in to each other's desires." This attitude survived for centuries. Love was an indulgence; marriage was linked importantly to economic and political life. When land, money, and power were involved, nothing so whimsical as love was considered a good basis for choosing a partner. Instead, marriage was built on practical motives and arranged in grittily realistic ways.

Historians tell us that the early American colonists were too preoccupied with building a nation to be romantic. Stendhal, the French novelist, commented after one of his visits. "Of the pleasure that passion gives, I see nothing." Under the harsh strictures of frontier life, a woman needed a man to support and defend her and a man needed a woman to take care of his physical needs and to give him children. Love was simply not a consideration.

Not until shortly after the First World War—when the automobile ushered in a new era of personal freedom and the motion picture discovered the impact of romance —did love become an important factor in marriage. Today, of course, it is the single *most* important factor. A poll taken in 1966 reported that 76 per cent of the married couples questioned named "love" as one of the two major reasons for marrying. (The second reason—to have children—was named by only 24 per cent.) Ten years later, in 1976, when a psychologist asked 75,000 wives to evaluate the reasons for their decision to wed, "Love, love, love was far and away the front runner," she reported.[3] In some surveys more than 90 percent of those questioned ranked love as the most essential element in marriage.

But none of these polls and studies asked the respondents what they *meant* by love. Or, more crucial perhaps, what they expected love to provide in the way of emotional rewards.

"This is an important area of disappointment in married life," observes psychologist Aron Krich. "In courtship the words 'I love you'—which usually mean 'I think you're wonderful'—are taken for granted. They are good words to trade, for the fact that someone wonderful thinks *you* are wonderful makes you feel and act more wonderful still. But when said during courtship the words 'I love you' are more a magical incantation than a statement of fact. [The phrase] may mean 'I desire you' or 'I want you to desire me.' It may mean 'I accept you as you are' or it may be a plea: 'Please take me as I am.' . . . Perhaps it means 'I feel guilty about you and want to correct the wrongs you have suffered from others,' or, conversely, 'I want you to feel guilty about *me* and correct the wrongs *I* have suffered at the hands of others.' Two people rarely mean the same thing when they say 'I love you.' In the reality of married life one comes face to face with what the other really meant. And that confrontation can be seriously disappointing."[4]

"I LOVE YOU, BUT I'M NOT IN LOVE WITH YOU"

Two people rarely mean the same thing when they say, "I love you." "Really? I never thought of it that way," say some. But even when we think of it, that insight does not at first seem particularly startling. We nod and say, "I suppose that's so." Yet until the new research which forms the underpinning of this book was begun, virtually no experts in interpersonal behavior had thought to investigate whether that actually was so, why it might be so, and what effect it might have on love relationships if indeed it were so. There was no informed knowledge, for example, as to what might happen to a couple who unwittingly tried to build a relationship on the basis of different understandings about the nature of love. Should one person seek to convince the other that his or her idea of love was the "right" one or the "better" one? And what happens when each expects the other to behave in certain ways in order to be considered "loving"?

The predictable outcomes include conflict, disappointment, and distress. Even more incongruous and disappointing is the discovery that one's own idea of what love is supposed to be or mean is questioned or demeaned. What happens when it no longer seems to make sense or to hold true in the relationship? In counseling with clients, therapists hear again and again the sometimes plaintive, sometimes desperate words, "I just don't love her anymore," or "I love him, but I'm not *in* love with him." This usually means that a particular quality the speaker seeks in love is missing or has changed. The client has a mental or emotional image of how he or she expects love to feel and to function; but despite the therapist's best efforts this image can seldom be made clear—largely because it was not clear to the client in the first place.

What *is* clear is that men and women mean something, even if they don't know exactly what, when they talk of love this way. And it follows that if one is supposed to feel or show love—whatever that means—then something must be done about it when those feelings—whatever they are—no longer are present.

One possible outcome is for the disappointed partner to make an emotional sacrifice, to give up the expectation that his or her particular idea of love can or should continue to exist. Newlyweds, for instance, frequently are admonished to remember that their current feelings of love will change to something "more mature." The implication is that their romantic and erotic feelings will fade and be replaced by something "better and more comfortable." It is true that some couples begin a relationship with the proverbial stars in their eyes—with an intensity of emotion that even *they* don't really expect to last. And yet when these intense feelings do moderate, the couple feel let down, disappointed.

One woman tells of a kind of intellectual conversion she made at this point: "I came to the conclusion that love really is not the glow and excitement I believed it to be when I was younger. Gradually, I convinced myself that *true* love is far more satisfying than the kind of infatuation I now know I was experiencing when I was first married." The woman had neatly—and correctly—changed her definition of love to make it fit the way her feelings had been changing. This is one of the important ways that we can deal with disappointment in love or anything else—we modify our thought processes to match both our new feelings and the reality of our situation.

A second major way to deal with disillusionment about love involves making an emotional compromise. Instead of changing our definition of love to fit the circumstances, we can decide to accept the circumstances as perhaps a watered-down form of love. We acknowledge that what we define as "love" may no longer be able to provide an enduring basis for the relationship; if we still want the relationship to continue, then something else—companionship, perhaps, or mere mutual tolerance—will have to replace it. In effect we give up being "in love" as either impractical or impossible. There is always the feeling that something is missing, but other factors—caring, concern, security—weigh more heavily. As one man put it: "I think about leaving my wife to find someone with whom I can really fall in love again. It's awfully depressing to know you'll never have that wonderful sensation any more. But then I tell myself that most love affairs don't last forever, that even if I find a new and exciting person our love will probably become routine after a time. Besides, I honestly care about my wife. She's good for me in many ways, and we get on well together. I think she feels the lack of romance or love in our life, too. But we have other things going for us, and our marriage isn't all that unpleasant. Actually, I guess it could be a lot worse."

For many men and women, however, redefining or compromising their ideas of love is not a good enough solution. They try to find the missing ingredients of their definition of love in other relationships. But to plunge into an affair, to risk or to seek separation and divorce, is an extreme way of dealing with conflicting attitudes toward love. Rather, we believe this reaction is the result of personality differences—whether a person is primarily "other oriented" or primarily concerned with his or her own welfare, or that of the partner's. It is not as easy as one might expect to detect the factors that spell the difference between those two attitudes. Consider the following conversation that took place in a counselor's office recently and see if you can decide which course of action this man will choose:

Husband: I'm not in love with my wife anymore, and I've been thinking of getting a divorce. Maybe that sounds cruel, but life is passing me by. I'm going to be forty-five years old next month and if I'm ever going to be happy I've got to leave and make a new life for myself!

Marcia Lasswell: I'm wondering, since you seem to feel so strongly about it, why you haven't already left?

Husband: Well, there are a lot of reasons. I'm worried about what my children will think of me if I divorce their mother . . . I don't want to lose their love. Then there's the financial side of it. I wouldn't have much money left to live on after I paid child support, and maybe some alimony. Then there are her parents. They've been more like my own, since I was never close to my family. It's only natural that they'll side with her and be angry at me. So you see, it isn't as easy for me to leave as you might think.

M.L.: It seems to me that your concerns are all for yourself . . . for the consequences that *you* would suffer in a divorce. I don't hear you speaking about the pain your wife and children or your in-laws would suffer except as it will affect you. You seem to look at everything with yourself at the center. I have the feeling that if you could find a way to minimize the effects on yourself you'd leave home right away.

And, indeed that is how this man finally did resolve his conflict. Those who evaluate cause and effect in this way are much more likely to make choices on the basis of their own personal happiness than on the basis of loyalty or responsibility to others.

DIFFERENCES

John and Vera have been husband and wife for forty-five years. They still remember clearly how they met, and how quickly they realized their love for each other. "We were married two months after I started courting her," John said. "It was love at first sight for both of us."

"When you look at Vera today, or when you think about

her," we asked, "do you still have the same feeling you had then?"

"Oh yes," John said. "I know that's difficult for some folks to believe, but that's just because it hasn't been that way for them. You have to experience love the way Vera and I know it in order to understand what it can really be like."

Another couple we talked with recently have lived together happily for eight years.

> "Almost everyone we know assumes Jan and I are husband and wife," says Dean, thirty-one years old, "because we are obviously devoted to each other. But I don't think we'll ever marry even though neither of us can imagine life without the other. But when you start talking about being 'in love,' I'm not sure I know what you mean. We care deeply for each other and we are sexually faithful. But bells don't ring, if that's what love is supposed to be like." Jan said: "Certainly we love each other. But neither of us wants the kind of romanticism or intenseness that being 'in love' seems to imply. We like what we have: a genuine caring relationship without all the complications of being 'in love'!"

Clearly, John and Vera would be mystified by Dean's and Jan's idea of love and they, in turn, would find the older couple's attitude quaintly sentimental. The fact is that accepting someone else's definition of love is extremely hard to do.

"We will accept variety in almost anything, from roses and religions to politics and poetry," writes John Alan Lee, a pioneer in research on how people love. "But when it comes to love, each of us believes we know the real thing, and we are reluctant to accept other notions. We disparage other people's experiences by calling them infatuations, mere sexual flings, delusions, unrealistic affairs."[5] Yet the more one studies love the more one discovers that there is no single "true" or "right" way in which it expresses itself, but many ways. This disturbs people who cling to the belief that there is—or at least should be—an unvarying definition that would pin love down once and for all, much as a beautiful butterfly is pinned and labeled on a display board. But love has always meant different things to different people. It is more than merely a matter of "different strokes for different folks." It involves deeply divergent and often sharply contradictory concepts of love.

Here is an example: A husband and wife enter counseling in hopes of finding a way to revive a marriage they describe as "spiraling downward into non-caring." As part of their therapy the counselor suggests that between office sessions the couple set aside a day, or part of a day, during which each spouse in turn will do whatever he or she thinks will please the other. (Marital therapists often give such "marital homework" to clients to encourage them to practice new and constructive ways of behaving toward each other.) In this case the couple agree that the wife will take her turn first one Sunday as the "caring" partner.

"She made a list of things that she felt I would like to have her do for me," the husband reported in a subsequent session with the therapist, "and I must admit that she went about each one with a good deal of enthusiasm and sincerity. She began the day by bringing me breakfast in bed. Then she ran a hot bath for me, and while I was in the tub she brought me a paperback novel she had bought because she thought I'd enjoy reading it. Then, as her big surprise, she produced a pair of tickets to an afternoon concert."

"And how did you feel about all that?" the therapist asked.

The man hesitated, then blurted out: "I didn't like it! I felt like a complete ingrate, of course, but I hated it. I do not like to have breakfast in bed; it makes me think I'm in a hospital. I much prefer a shower to a tub bath, and I certainly want to choose my own reading matter. As for the concert—well, I do enjoy music but it so happened there was a play-off football game on television that afternoon that I would rather have watched."

"So the experiment was a complete failure?" inquired the counselor.

"Not really," the man replied. "Halfway through the day I realized something important. All the things my wife did for me were things she would have wanted me to do for *her*. I suddenly understood what would make *her* feel loved. For the first time I started to know the difference between what she really wanted from me and what I *thought* she wanted."

In this instance the "caring" experiment, artificial though

it was, produced important insights. In most relationships,
however, partners remain unaware that their ways of dem-
onstrating and accepting love are incompatible. The emotional script is obvious, and self-defeating:

> I, like every man and woman, want to be loved. But, like
> every man and woman, I have my own idea, grounded
> in my personality and temperament and experience, of
> what loving and being loved means. Moreover, locked
> in the prison of my own ways of thinking and feeling, I
> assume that my definition of love is the only correct one.
> As a result, I want and expect to be loved in the same
> way that I love others, with the same responses that I
> interpret as the evidence of lovingness.
>
> But I am *not* loved that way. Instead (and quite logi-
> cally, if one could be logical about this), I am loved the
> way my *partner* thinks and feels about love, the way he
> or she understands and expresses it. In my own distress,
> I do not recognize that my partner is experiencing the
> same incongruity in reverse. Puzzled, hurt, unable to
> communicate our confusion to each other, we both un-
> reasonably feel unloved.

FINDING COMPATIBLE STYLES OF LOVE

Compatibility is a basic force that gives strength and
steadiness to a love relationship. There are those who believe that being compatible can hold a couple together
even though passion and romance may have departed the
scene. There is a tendency to think of compatibility as a
substitute for love—a sort of low-keyed attachment based
on shared values and mutually agreeable ways of living.
But we have come to believe that compatibility, much
more than a pale proxy for love, is one of three essential
factors that comprise an individual's potential for happiness in his or her love life.

The first factor is internal: the mental, physical, and
psychological structures that make up personality and thus
help lay the basis for the way one feels and thinks about
love. The second factor is external: environmental forces
such as jobs, friends, daily experiences—and the love relationship itself—that help to shape the ways in which one
shows love and expects to receive it. Compatibility is the
third factor, for it determines the degree to which each

partner's definition of love—a definition formed by the other two factors—will be in harmony.

There are six basic ways in which people define and express their concept of love—six styles of loving. They are not necessarily mutually exclusive. Indeed, most of us love in ways that combine two or more of these styles although one style is usually dominant. Since each of us has had a different set of growing-up experiences, it is not surprising that each of us should have a unique definition of what love means. What is surprising is that the existence of individual love styles has for so long been denied.

Most couples have little difficulty learning how to adapt to or adjust to each other's styles of eating, sleeping, working, playing. We aren't unduly distressed when our partner turns out to prefer sleeping on his or her stomach while we prefer sleeping on our side. We are not ready to call the relationship a failure if he or she likes to have salad before the main course while we like to have it afterward. But most of us are not nearly so tolerant of the similar differences which exist in individual ways of loving. We are distressed when they become apparent, and we are often ready to call the relationship a failure if the differences persist or cannot be bridged.

How, then, can couples learn to love each other the way each partner wants and needs to be loved?

First, by realizing that there *are* differences in love styles. Second, by learning to identify these styles, to know one's own and one's partner's. Third, by understanding how these styles manifest themselves in giving and receiving love. And by developing the skill of meshing styles that may be in conflict with each other. There are no rules for making these continuing, flexible, and empathetic adjustments. Aldous Huxley may have described the process best when he wrote: "There isn't any formula for loving. You learn to love . . . by paying attention and doing what one thereby discovers has to be done."

2

HOW WE LEARN TO LOVE

And we are put on earth . . .
That we may learn to . . . love.
—William Blake, *Songs of Innocence*

By the time we are eighteen or nineteen years old most of
us have been "in love" at least once and, according to
research findings, probably two or three times.[1] No one
considers this a sign of emotional precocity. After all,
aren't we simply doing "what comes naturally"? Almost no
human activity save breathing is assumed to be more spontaneous or unpremeditated than falling in love. But if that
is true, what accounts for the mess we so often make of
it? "There is hardly any enterprise which is started with
such tremendous hopes and expectations, and yet, which
fails so regularly, as love," writes Erich Fromm.[2] To overcome this pattern of failure, he said, men and women must
realize that love is an art. However, before one can effectively pursue the art of love one must, in the first place,
learn *to* love.

Discovering and developing the capacity to give and receive feelings of love is a fascinating emotional adventure.
Like any other aptitude or skill, love is learned through
example, imitation, and practice. Every person who becomes involved in a love relationship brings to it the lifelong history of his or her experiences with others. Many
of these experiences are stored as conscious memories;
many others become assimilated into the unconscious in a
mixture of feelings, sentiments, predispositions, and prej-
udices. How these influences combine to affect us determines what we think and feel about loving—how we want
to *be* loved and how we *show* love— throughout life. Thus
each person's style of loving is largely a product of his or
her past, an amalgam of plusses and minuses that gov-

ern one's needs for love as well as one's ability to give
love.

LOVE'S BEGINNINGS

The potential for loving exists from the moment of birth.
Some even say it is an inborn urge. Babies, in the first days
and even hours of life, display love's fundamental pattern:
they respond in a positive way toward whoever fulfills
their needs. This is called "approach behavior," and in one
way or another it appears in virtually all newborn animals.
In the human baby it takes the form of an intense attraction for the nurturing parents.

This attraction is essentially the earliest, most primitive
form of love. At first it is motivated by the infant's struggle
to survive. In the womb, necessities such as warmth, protection, nourishment, and elimination were provided automatically. Now the baby must rely for these and other essential supplies and services on the good will of other persons. The baby manages this change successfully by turning dependency into an asset. This evokes those feelings
of affection and protection that are programmed into human emotional circuits and triggered by the presence of a
small, helpless, appealing creature—a kitten, a puppy, a
baby. "To be loved, be lovable," advised Ovid. His counsel
was for those who sought romantic or erotic success; but
babies seem to know how to use that technique for their
own goals.

When a parent responds to an infant's survival demands
we call it "mother love" (even though nowadays much of
this nurturing function is performed by fathers as well).
Mother love—and, springing from it, all love—is an in-
vention of the mammal. Experts on brain evolution point
out that reptiles ignore or even devour their offspring. The
development of the parenting impulse, however, occurred
with the development of the early mammalian brain, known
as the limbic system.[3] When it is damaged, or removed in
animal experiments, mothering behavior is disturbed. In
this "emotional brain," says the experts, are the evolu-
tionary roots of love.

If asked to analyze mother love we usually tend to describe it as "mature" or "selfless" since it seems to consist
mainly of satisfying another's needs. And it is true that for
a while this burgeoning "love affair" between baby and

parents is one-sided. The infant is not aware that mother and father are love objects. He or she knows only that food appears when it is needed, that diapers are changed when they cause discomfort, that being cuddled feels good. In the earliest months of life it does not matter to the baby who performs these chores; almost anyone—mother, father, grandparent, sitter—will do.

Yet in one sense the baby's behavior can accurately be described as loving. Not, of course, purposefully or even consciously. But the result is much the same. Simply by becoming a visible, tangible individual—a real person with a unique personality—after the long months of being a "mysterious stranger" in the womb, an infant can be a psychological source of love to the parents. Moreover, a loving and need-fulfilling interaction between baby and parents begins immediately after birth. A baby permitted to nurse at the mother's breast as soon as he is born, observes psychiatrist Roderic Gorney, obtains "antibodies, vitamins and minerals, while he stimulates . . . the womb contractions that deliver the afterbirth, stop bleeding, and prevent afterpains. In this mutual giving is born synergically the bond of affection that ties the new baby to others for the rest of his life." In short, says Gorney, "We are biologically predisposed to loving interdependence. . . ."[4]

Laboratory experiments have proved that this is not sentimental theorizing. For example, researchers using thermal photography techniques to measure changes in blood flow have shown that an infant's cry stimulates blood circulation in the nipples, thereby increasing the secretion of milk.[5] The infant's ability to cling and to nuzzle communicates a pleasurable warmth to the parent. At Harvard, where pediatrician Dr. T. Berry Brazelton is studying early mother-infant interaction, slow-motion photography reveals that mother and baby unconsciously "tune in and out" to each other's cycles of babbling, smiling, and touching. "Underlying all this rhythmic cycling of attention and recovery," says Dr. Brazelton, "is a very important mechanism called a 'feedback' system. My colleagues and I see this as the base of the baby's earliest ability to communicate emotionally. . . . As the mother and baby respond to each other's rhythms, they are saying to each other that they are really in touch, that they are really locked in to each other."[6]

Indeed, use of the phrase "in touch" is no semantic accident. Touching is a crucial aspect of all human relationships. As the main avenue by which the need for intimacy is satisfied, skin contact is biologically essential to an infant. For this reason, perhaps, the nerve fibers that connect the skin to the central nervous system are the most highly developed organs in the newborn baby's boby. (Nor is this phenomenon limited to human babies. In a series of famous experiments psychologist Dr. Harry Harlow some years ago separated monkey babies from their mothers and substituted "dummy" mothers. One was built out of a bare wire frame, and another of sponge rubber covered with terry cloth. Both had wooden heads and artificial breasts. In half of each set of "mothers" a contraption enabled milk to be suckled through the breasts. Though it had always been assumed that the satisfaction of suckling was the prime cause of emotional attachment between infants and mothers, Harlow's monkey babies all became attached to the terry-cloth dummies, whether or not they were equipped to give milk. The infant monkeys spent hours clinging to the terry-cloth frames for the pleasure of physical contact alone.)[7]

Even more significant in the development of human love is Brazelton's finding that if a mother "disappoints" her baby by falling out of step with his or her response cycle —say, by maintaining a sober and expressionless face while the child tries to get her to smile or to play—the infant first grows concerned, then anxious. Ultimately the baby withdraws, face turned aside, body curled up and motionless. She may even go to sleep to "defend" herself from this lack of a loving response. What these behaviors indicate, Brazelton feels, is that even an infant less than a month old expects positive emotional responses from her parents and has strong ways of defending herself against disappointment when these do not occur. Thus a baby learns, says Brazelton, "about being loved, and [about] some of the limits on it."[8]

In turn, the infant's evident satisfaction when his or her needs *are* met is a response that makes the parents feel loved. So, rather than being merely an emotional sponge who does nothing but demand and absorb love, a baby is a source and provider of love as well. This interaction between parent and child forms the basis for the fundamental definition of love as a strong need or desire to be close to another person who will supply our physical and emotional needs. The novelist Balzac put it more poetically. Love, he wrote, is "the warmth of gratitude that all generous souls feel for the source of their pleasures."

True emotional attachment develops when an infant nears six months of age. At this stage the baby recognizes the one or two persons who supply most of his or her wants and has special feelings for them. The presence of the loved ones themselves now means as much to the baby as the physical comfort they give. The bonds of love are still based on needs, to be sure, but the fact that only special people can truly satisfy them is the beginning of what will grow, in time, to be the feelings we call love. Now when the baby is held he or she reaches out, responds with touch or smile to gestures, voice tones, body rhythms. These comprise the language of love long before "I love you" can be spoken. Indeed, the very fact that a baby has no way of labeling with words what he experiences causes a very special and important kind of learning to take place: emotional learning. That is why, when these preverbal memories swim up into consciousness in our adult years, they so often take the form of visual images or tantalizing recollections of a certain taste or touch or odor.

A man, thirty-three: Sometimes I see a woman, a stranger, who has a particular shade of blond hair, ash blond I would describe it now, and suddenly I seem to recall my mother coming to kiss me good night, her blond hair tickling my face. But how could I remember that? My mother died before I was three years old!

A woman, forty-six: Ever since I can remember, my father used a special shaving lotion. Today, when I catch a whiff of that aroma I am lifted up on a wave of loving feelings. It's as if I am enveloped in a kind of love I can't put into words.

Such feelings cannot be put into words precisely because they are cued by sense-memories of experiences that occurred before language was available to us. They can often be lifelong influences.

EARLY MODELS—HOW PARENTS TEACH ABOUT LOVE

If emotions are "contagious"—anger sparking anger, fear evoking fear, jealousy kindling jealousy—then love seems to be no exception. One of the most important influences on the way we learn to love is the model our parents provide. How *they* love us teaches us how to love others. We learn to love by the way we ourselves are loved.

Parents teach love by the way they respond to a child's early attempts to reach out for it. We have only to think of two people in love—their caressing, kissing, even the way they express their feelings in baby talk—to see how closely they resemble parents and children being affectionate together. The tender words and loving touches experienced in childhood have prepared the couple to respond to each other as adults in much the same way. Children who miss that experience in their formative years may find it awkward at best, and impossible at worst, to give and to receive that kind of loving behavior in later life. In one instance a family concerned about a teen-age son's rebelliousness consulted a therapist. The counselor spent weeks seeking to restore some kind of communication between the emotionally estranged boy and his father. Suddenly one day, in the midst of an argument, the father stood up and impulsively embraced his son. The boy hugged back, and both began to cry. "This is the first time I can remember your holding me," the boy said. "I always wanted to," the man replied. "Believe me, I wanted to . . . but somehow I was afraid, I couldn't bring myself to do it."

Another powerful lesson in love is provided by the way parents express, or fail to express, love for each other. How mother and father feel about and act toward each other is for most people a basic model of a love relationship. It is the one we can observe most closely and over the longest period of time. Since children learn important lessons by imitation, they frequently adopt as their own love style the kind of love behavior they see their parents use.

This may be positive, but any therapist's office can furnish tragic proof of this as well. Recently a husband and wife came to Marcia Lasswell for help with what they said, at first, was a sexual problem:

Husband: There's really more to it than just the sex part. My wife doesn't even like for me to touch her any time.
Wife: That's because it always means you want to go to bed! You always have sex on your mind.
Husband: That just isn't true. How can I have sex on my

mind when you're fixing dinner and the children are right there? I just like to touch, and you don't. You don't understand what it means.

M.L. (to husband): Tell me about your parents, Ted. Were they physically affectionate toward each other?

Husband: Oh yes. Everyone in our family touches a lot. I often saw my parents hugging and kissing. It gave me a good feeling to know they loved each other. But Jackie's family is quite different. They are always stiff and formal, even with each other. It's as if any physical contact is something to be ashamed of.

M.L. (to wife): Is that an accurate description?

Wife: Pretty much. I don't think I ever saw my parents kiss or hug. They must have made love often enough to have four children, but they certainly didn't let any of us see them being affectionate.

M.L.: And what about their touching or cuddling you children? Was there much of that?

Wife: Almost none that I can recall. Oh, sometimes my father would give me a kiss when he came home from work, but it was as if he was embarrassed about doing it. And they never said anything affectionate to us, either. Ted says my family is the original "stiff-upper-lip" club. I can even remember my mother speaking with disdain of a sister-in-law who always kissed her when they came to visit.

M.L.: I wonder, Jackie, if you somehow grew to believe that touching always has sexual overtones? Children who grow up in homes where there is a lot of open physical affection learn to distinguish clearly between sexual and non-sexual touching. But you may not have learned that difference.

Wife (doubtful): Maybe not. I'll have to admit that when Ted touches me I immediately assume he's leading up to something.

M.L.: And if you believe Ted always wants sex when he touches you—and if he does this several times a day—you could feel he has a one-track mind?

Wife: Exactly. That's why I feel angry and almost cringe physically every time he comes near me.

Husband: Which makes me feel like a creep! And it really puzzles me, because Jackie liked sex when we were first together.

M.L.: Jackie may still like sex. But she needs to find a way to understand when your touching is sexual and when it is just affectionate. You grew up knowing the difference, but she has to learn it. Jackie, it's possible that touching will never have the same meaning for you as it does for Ted. People who grow up as "touchers" have a real hunger for skin contact. But you can certainly learn to respond differently to different kinds of touches. This is not going to be easy for you to do. And, Ted, you will have to be sensitive to your wife's lack of need or desire for fewer physical signs of affection than you seem to need or want. If you can both work on that successfully, I'm sure we'll see a change in Jackie's sexual responsiveness as a result.

A person's attitude toward love, and toward the way it is expressed, tends to be a direct result of such childhood experiences. For example, the mother of a now adult son recalls that when her boy was growing up she lavished affection upon him openly. "Today he always gives his father and me a hug and kiss whenever he sees us," she says. "And he is warm and tender with his wife and with his own children. People used to tell me I was spoiling him by giving him so much love. I don't think that's possible."

On the other hand, parental love may be bewilderingly inconsistent, and thus teach quite a different lesson.

"I never knew what to expect from my dad," a thirty-six-year-old bachelor states. "Sometimes he'd come home from work and roughhouse with me, or take me out into the yard for a game of catch before dinner. Other times he'd walk into the house and when I would run up to hug him he'd growl and tell me to leave him alone. After a while I decided it was best not to show my feelings, not to commit myself. I'd learned how disappointing it is to be rejected."

That caution, instilled during childhood, may be the chief reason this man has never married. To grow up believing it is not safe to put emotional trust in others can cause one to avoid any intimacy that seems likely to arouse the old fears.

"HOW MANY TIMES DO I HAVE
TO TELL YOU ... ?"

"You cannot love another person unless you love your-self." Most people have heard that statement so often they tend to dismiss it as just another catch phrase in the lexicon of pop psychology. But a solid sense of self-esteem—that amorphous but significant quality that determines whether we feel "good" or "bad" about ourselves—is a vital element in building the capacity to love.[9]

The creation of a positive or negative self-image begins in infancy. A parent smiles or frowns, says, "Bad boy!" or "Good girl!", applauds the early awkward efforts to use a spoon and drink from a cup or impatiently slaps the hand that drops the utensil and shouts, "Now look at the mess you made!" Each of these and thousands of similar experiences may be permanently filed in our intellectual and emotional memory banks. There they form a storehouse of impressions on which we draw, all through life, to feel good or bad about ourselves.

For most people, it would seem, these memory banks are unfortunately crammed with childhood incidents that left them feeling belittled or rejected. Dr. Honor Whitney, a family therapist who for many years has been studying the effects of destructive and supportive remarks made to youngsters, asked groups of men and women to reminisce about this aspect of their early years. One man declared he would never forget a phrase his parents repeatedly said to him: "Whenever I did anything they considered wrong or stupid they would say, 'How many times do I have to tell you . . . ?' It made me feel like a hopeless failure, a horrible boy not deserving of their love."

As social animals, all men and women seek and need approval from those around them. The way each of us comes to feel about himself or herself reflects in large part the way other people respond to us. The good opinion of those closest to us (usually family members) is especially significant. It is from their words and actions that we draw a self-portrait that shows whether we see ourselves as competent or useless, worthy or unworthy of respect, likable or obnoxious, a success or a failure—in short, as either a lovable or an unlovable person. For example,

Evelyn is a slim, attractive, twenty-six-year-old medical technician.

"What I remember most vividly from my childhood," she says, "is being teased by my family about my height. My dad always called me 'skyscraper' and my brother called me 'F.L.' for foot-long, because he said I looked like a skinny frankfurter. I know they didn't mean to be cruel, but by the time I was fifteen I was convinced I was a gangly freak and no boy would ever want to date me. It took years before I had any confidence with men. Even now I tower over them. I try not to go out with any man who isn't several inches taller than I am. But tall men seem to prefer cuddly, shorter girls."

Since those who have a poor self-image think themselves unworthy of love, they often are unable to accept it. "How can I love someone," a woman asks—and means it—"who has no better sense than to love me?" A man recalls that whenever his mother was annoyed with him she would say, despairingly: "I just don't like the way you *are!*" "I never understood what she meant by that," he says. "What was I supposed to do about it?" He still does not know what to do about it, for whenever a woman seems to like him he backs away from her. He has such a poor image of himself as a lovable person that he assumes any woman capable of falling in love with him—of liking the way he is—cannot be worth very much herself.

CONDITIONAL LOVE

The use of love as a reward or a punishment is another very real factor in determining how we learn to love. Many youngsters implicitly learn that love is conditional —given almost literally "on approval" when they please a parent and withheld when they do not. "I knew my parents loved me no matter what I did" is the remark of a person who was loved absolutely, with no strings and no expectation of return. In such a home even punishment is meted out in a spirit of caring. But "I knew I had to get good grades and behave myself properly if I wanted my parents to love me" is the remark of a person who has learned that love may be a device for exerting control over another. Several widely used psychological tests pose open-ended sentences that the respondent must complete. A typical sentence is: "I felt that my parents loved me most when I . . ." A surprisingly large number of people report that *some* kind of "approved" behavior was necessary to evoke a loving response:

". . . helped my mother clean the house."
". . . stayed out of trouble in school."
". . . brought them presents."
". . . smiled a lot and looked pretty."

Another incomplete sentence, "I felt my parents loved me least when I . . ." brought these typical replies:

". . . fought with my sister."
". . . got bad marks."
". . . talked back."
". . . didn't go to church."

What is most significant is the fact that only a handful of men and women had trouble recalling a time when they felt least loved. Clearly the conditional withholding of love is a technique used frequently to establish authority or to control behavior. Is it any wonder that so many of us grow to fear, in later life, that love may be withdrawn whenever we do not please the persons whose love we cherish? Is it any wonder that we come to accept the idea that we ourselves have the right to withdraw love when *we* are displeased with them?

So powerful is the need to give and receive love, however, that it perseveres in the face of all but total rejection. There are isolated instances of children—abandoned, shuttled from foster home to foster home, perhaps institutionalized at an early age—who never are able to establish the primary bonding experience that would enable them, later in life, to love others, or to feel they themselves are worthy of being loved. But this total lack of attachment, this complete failure to learn how to love, is extremely rare. Even when a baby or young child is grossly neglected or abused, the "approach" circuits do not shut down. Children of the most withdrawn, unloving or physically abusive parents continue to seek love from them. Even when they are adults some of these emotionally deprived men and women still keep hoping to earn parental approval and affection. Our concern, then, is not so much with the few who cannot love at all as it is with those who learn troubled or distorted ways of loving and seeking love.

For example, when the need for emotional attachment is unfulfilled in childhood it sometimes sets in motion a lifelong search for "someone to love." Not long ago a seventeen-year-old girl, a part-time model and a part-time prostitute, was murdered in Los Angeles, the victim of a strangler who preyed on rootless young women. Police investigation revealed that the girl's mother had deserted her in infancy and her father had been killed when she was not quite nine years old. At thirteen she ran away from another in a long series of foster homes to search for her mother and, as a relative said later: "She kept running, searching for love, some sort of love, any sort of love. Maybe she thought the life she chose was the only way she could find it."

TOO LITTLE AND TOO MUCH

Psychologists talk of such persons and such families as "love-poor." They are characterized more by emotional apathy than by antipathy. In their households warmth and affection—not only between parents and children but also between the spouses themselves—are usually scantily displayed or missing entirely. In such homes children are doubly short-changed: they do not get sufficient love, and they have no models for learning how to get it or to give it. Studies reveal that members of "love-poor" families have several characteristics in common:

• They are less happy than men and women who grow up in families where love is openly displayed and shared.
• They place a low value on love as a significant aspect of life.
• They value money as a source of happiness far more than those who grow up in loving families, and emphasize material possessions as substitutes for love.
• They seem to feel that love has no part to play in their lives. As a result they devalue it, and often try to avoid situations and relationships in which love might be found.[10]

Paradoxically, however, too much love—or what is intended as love—can be almost as damaging as too little. For instance, children who grow up with oversolicitous parents who go to extreme lengths to meet every emotional need may become overly dependent. When they seek love later in life they may find themselves psychologically fixated at this "infantile" stage of bonding. Of course, remnants of loving behavior caused by emotional neediness may exist in the most mature persons. For instance, most of us at one time or another feel unloved when a partner does not fulfill a request. The pattern of infantile bonding has taught us that a parent—or anyone — who loves us will always meet our needs. And so we revert to the childish notion that "you would do this for me if you really love me."

But if we do not move *beyond* this fixation we may desperately seek a partner who seems likely to cater to our whims at any cost. Any deviation, any rejection, may cause us to feel unloved and, possibly, unlovable. Those who become trapped in this stage—loving someone out of need rather than needing someone out of love—tend to be constantly apprehensive and often fearful of being alone. Too emotionally dependent to make a wise choice of partner, they usually "fall in love" with anyone who promises to take care of them. More often than not the choice is wrong. Instead of finding a nurturant parent substitute, these men and women may find themselves in a situation in which they must take a great deal of the bad to get a crumb or two of the good that is so acutely important to them.

Dorothy was such a victim of love dependency. She was referred for marital therapy when she confided to her physician that her husband had beaten her. It soon became clear that this was not the first time. In fact, there had been incidents of physical violence before they were married. But Dorothy was so emotionally dependent that she felt she had to put up with whatever her husband did simply to keep him living with her.

Marcia Lasswell: I'm wondering why you married him when you already knew he was capable of violence toward you?
Dorothy: I guess I thought once we were married he

wouldn't be so jealous. That's what caused the beatings many times.

M.L.: Do you give him any reason to be jealous?

Dorothy: I've never even looked at another man. Besides, what man would be interested in me?

M.L.: Why do you say that?

Dorothy: I've never had much success attracting men. I never even dated much before I met Bill. He was the first guy who ever paid attention to me that way.

M.L.: And when he was jealous, what did that mean to you?

Dorothy: That he loved me, I guess. He *said* he did, anyway. And he promised me what I had always wanted and longed for.

M.L.: What was that?

Dorothy: Well . . . security, I guess, and love. You see, when I met Bill, I was living away from home for the first time. I was lonely and scared. My parents and I had always been very close and I missed them terribly.

M.L.: And Bill promised to take care of you?

Dorothy: Exactly, I fell head over heels in love. I didn't want him out of my sight for a minute.

M.L.: And even though violence came with the package, you've stayed with him?

Dorothy (after long silence): I'm afraid to be alone.

M.L.: You are paying a high price for what you are getting, aren't you?

Dorothy: I guess I never think of it in that way. But what can I do about it now?

M.L.: We have only two options, really. One is to help you learn to be less dependent, less desperate for someone to replace your lost parents. You can't recapture the kind of relationship you had with them. Instead, you need to learn to love yourself more so you won't feel that you have to put up with physical abuse in order to hold onto your husband. Our other option is to work with you and Bill as a couple, to see whether he can change, too, once he understands his own motivations better.

One of the most significant steps in learning to love maturely is the achievement of emotional independence from one's parents. Dorothy had failed to do this. But only then would she be able to view a love partner from the perspective of an adult's identity rather than from the identity of a still love-needy child.

This process of becoming emotionally independent of parents begins, if all goes well, at a surprisingly early age. By the first birthday a child has already started to learn that, while Mommy and Daddy can be counted upon when they are needed, it is not catastrophic to be alone for a while. The concept of emotional trust has been introduced. Even if loved ones disappear for brief periods the child is reassured by the knowledge—based on experience —that they will indeed return. Meanwhile, there are love substitutes: a grandparent, a familiar sitter, an older brother or sister, even a favorite stuffed animal or security blanket. They are a comfort during the parents' absence. We can see traces of similar behavior in adults when a picture of the loved one, a lock of hair, a phone call, or a letter serves as a reassuring link during separations. A youngster who has been well loved during the first crucial period of dependency is able to develop the security that's needed in order to tolerate increasing amounts of independence. He or she can gradually allow emotional space between himself or herself and loved ones. This second stage of learning how to love is as vital as the primary bonding stage. It is the foundation of that delicate balance between separateness and togetherness that enables two adult lovers to be emotionally close and yet retain their individuality. It is the basis of the knowledge that we can merge intimately with a lover without having to fear that we will be overwhelmed by him or her, trapped in a dependency we simultaneously seek and resent. Some children do not make this transition successfully, either because their parents are so distant there is never the opportunity to build up trust, or because their parents are so overly close there is never the chance to learn to tolerate separateness.

OTHER "TEACHERS" OF LOVE— SIBLINGS, PEERS, SOCIETY

Though we may have made it seem as if parents deserve all the credit (or all the blame) for how we learn (or fail to learn) to love, they are not our only teachers. Parents exert a basic and powerful influence, obviously. But many other persons and factors have an increasingly important effect as children pass beyond the preschool years.

Siblings. The antagonisms and jealousies among brothers and sisters have been well documented. Not so well realized is the fact that the positive feelings that exist among them play a part in the development of loving behavior. As adults, we often choose love partners who remind us in important ways of our opposite-sex siblings. Or we may reenact in an adult love relationship the kind of behavior we learned to use with a brother or sister. Indeed, what psychologists call "birth order"—the sequence in which we and our siblings are born—can have a lifelong effect on our feelings and actions.

Certainly birth order plays a significant role in shaping personality. An only child, for instance, tends to feel he or she is "special." Because "onlys" spend most of their time with adults (and because parents have more time and energy to give to an only child), an only child is usually more intelligent and articulate and is quick to adopt adult values. Because an "only" never has to compete with a sibling for love or possessions, he or she is not likely to become highly competitive or demanding, but an only child does get used to being the center of attention.

Oldest children have some of the same qualities (after all, they too are "onlys" for a while), but they tend to grow jealous and competitive when siblings come along and push them out of their favored place. One way an oldest child tries to keep the major share of parental love is to be hardworking and conscientious. He or she also learns to take some of the responsibility for caring for the younger siblings. The youngest child—the permanent "baby" in the family—feels emotionally secure and is often most creative. But a youngest usually receives so much doting care, and gets used to being told what to do by so many different family members, that he or she may tend to become overly dependent. A middle child often feels left out, overlooked, and as a result learns either to fight for his or her rights or to develop the skills of tact and diplomacy. Of course, if a middle child is the opposite sex from the other siblings, this gives him or her a special distinction that eliminates the "middle-child syndrome." To be the sole son or daughter in a family can give one the same V.I.P. feeling that being an only child does.

Moreover, the order of birth results in a youngster's taking—or being "assigned"—a certain role in the family. Parents tend to identify an oldest child as the "responsible" one, a youngest as the "carefree" or "easygoing" one, and a middle child as the "unselfish" one, ready (or pressured) to yield to the siblings on either side. Eventually a child begins to think of himself or herself in those terms and to behave accordingly. "Inevitably," writes clinical psychologist Dr. Lucille Forer, an expert on birth order, "we carry these attitudes into the world outside the home and into adult life." Their impact affects not only the way we deal with daily circumstances but how we come to think of love, the kind of person we choose to love and marry, and the way we respond to the demands and rewards of love relationships. For instance, we often find it more natural to love someone who allows us to continue our childhood roles.[11] Here are two examples:

Kathy was looking forward to an evening out with her husband—dinner and a movie. She had done her hair and arranged for a sitter. But when Jim got home he asked Kathy if she would mind terribly if they didn't go out that night. "I'm absolutely beat," he said. "Three bigwigs from the home office were on my back all day, and they are going to be there first thing in the morning, too. I know I promised, but will you take a rain check for next week?"

At first Kathy felt keenly let down. Jim had disappointed her this way more than once lately. But she saw the tension and weariness in her husband's face and kept her disappointment to herself.

"I'll cancel the sitter," she said, "and fix something simple to eat. You relax. I'll hold you to that rain check, though." Her husband smiled. "You're terrific, honey," he said.

In the second instance Helen was also anticipating an evening out. She and her husband had been invited to a dinner party. But when Tom returned from a hectic business trip and said he was too exhausted to go anywhere Helen made a scene about it:

"I've been here alone all week, but you never think of me or my pleasure," she said resentfully. "You go off on those trips and see people and eat out in fancy restaurants, and then you won't do the simplest thing so that I can enjoy myself." Rather than get into an argument, or have Helen sulking about for days, Tom gave in and dragged himself to the party.

There are, of course, several possible reasons why the two women reacted so differently to essentially similar situations. But the factor of birth order was significant. Kathy had been the first-born child in her family, and she had two younger brothers whom she had always mothered and indulged. As a wife, her concept of loving behavior was still to be of help and comfort to the man in her life. Significantly, too, Jim was the youngest of four children and had been "babied" well into his teens. He may have sensed from the time he first met his wife that she was the sort of woman from whom he could expect the same sort of tender loving care. On the other hand, Helen was an only child whose parents had devoted themselves to her single-mindedly. She was, as a result, still emotionally fixated on having her own desires met and her own plans accepted. She found it difficult to adjust to the needs of other people—even those she loved. She believed that "if you love me you will do what I want." Her husband had been one of the two middle children in a family of four siblings. He had learned early in life that compromise could save him a good deal of trouble in the long run. His way of showing love was to give in.

Many men and women unconsciously seek to reconstruct in their adult lives much the same kinds of emotional relationships they experienced with siblings in childhood. A woman who grew up with three older brothers who treated her like a little princess married a wealthy man considerably older than herself. Another woman who grew up in a family of five close-knit siblings divorced her first husband, an only child, and married a man who had six brothers and sisters. "One of the reasons my first marriage broke up was my feeling of loneliness," she said. "Bill was content to read or listen to music for hours. I needed more activity, more contact with people. In my new marriage all the in-laws visit back and forth every weekend, holidays are a madhouse, and I thrive on it! It's like being part of a big, loving family again."

Peers. As a child moves into the wider arena beyond the home, peers and friends come to play a larger part in forming attitudes about love. One of the pioneers of psychotherapy, Harry Stack Sullivan, called the years from eight to twelve the "chum" period, when boys become fast friends with boys, and girls are often inseparable. Sullivan felt this stage was vital in the development of one's capacity to care for another person as much as one cares for oneself. But even quite young children have thoughts and feelings about what they call "love."[12]

Dr. Carlfred Broderick, one of America's leading family sociologists, found that when, say, an eight-year-old boy gives a birthday gift to another boy, or a girl gives a gift to a girl, it is done in a brisk, matter-of-fact way. But when a boy gives a gift to a girl, or vice versa, the procedure is accompanied by much giggling and coyness. "They behave for all the world as if they have crushes on each other," Broderick observed. Intrigued, he carried out more studies of six- to twelve-year-olds. He found that nine out of ten youngsters said they had "special" friends of the opposite sex. About half claimed to have "sweethearts" whom they said they "loved." In the early teen years boys and girls tend to fantasize love relationships. A boy may see himself as the hero of a "Robinson Crusoe" situation: isolated on a desert island with the girl he "loves," he will build a shelter, hunt and fish for food, protect her from wild animals; she will cook, mend clothes and utensils, and in general live up to preliberation stereotypes of "woman's role." A young girl will often engage in a "Tarzan and Jane" or "Pierre and Marie Curie" fantasy in which she and a beloved partner work together against great odds to achieve some beautiful or important goal. At this stage of development the idea of love for both boys and girls seems to be a fanciful imagery, an end in itself quite distinct from any sexual overtones. What seems to be the most likely scenario, experts now believe, is that children progress through a series of steps in learning how to love and that each step is preparation for the next. The first meaningful love relationship occurs for the first time in later adolescence.

*   *   *

Society. This is the final and most pervasive source of our lessons in loving. If we did not learn about love from parents, siblings, and peers, we would certainly learn about it from the society in which we live. Songs, motion pictures, television, books, magazines, advertisements—all make their often contradictory and confusing contribution to our impressions of what love is, what love should be, how it starts, how it feels, how it ends, and, perhaps most significant, how we are supposed to think and behave when we are in love. No wonder most men and women are bewildered when their ideas of love fail to jibe with the reality of their emotional lives. No wonder most of us are puzzled when our ways of showing love are not seen or accepted as loving behavior by our partners.

Love, then, is a learned response. It may seem to take us by surprise, to appear magically or mysteriously, to cause ecstasies or agonies we may not be able rationally to explain. But, at root, love is a set of feelings and a pattern of actions that we have learned. If we have been fortunate in our teachers, each love relationship from infancy onward is a step in the direction of personal growth.

If we are lucky, our early experiences of love produce good feelings: positive comforts as well as the relief of fears and anxieties. And as these experiences are repeated and these feelings reinforced over time, they become inextricably linked in our minds with the persons who make them possible. Their presence now is the signal for pleasure and for hope. Similarly, each new stage of development makes its contribution until, finally, we form our unique conception of that combination of attitudes and sensations that makes us feel loved, and the combination that makes us feel *un*loved.

But since this process involves so many thousands of learning experiences, so many scores of models of loving behavior, plus a whole cultural environment filled with suggestions and instructions as to what love is or ought to be—the result is that each of us arrives at a somewhat different idea of love. What we refer to as an individual's love "style"—romantic or practical, demanding or unselfish, trusting or manipulative—emerges from this sum total of how and what we learned.

When two partners have matching or dovetailing styles of love, result: happiness; when the styles are at odds with each other, result: conflict. Still, the fact that love *is* learned contains its own measure of hope. *For what is learned can be unlearned.* New and more congruent patterns of loving behavior can ultimately be developed to help each person achieve a more rewarding love relationship.

3

WHY COUPLES CHOOSE
EACH OTHER

> In literature as in love we are astonished at what
> is chosen by others.
>
> —André Maurois

Some months ago we attended the wedding of a friend's daughter. As the bride walked down the aisle toward her waiting groom a freak of acoustics in the arched chapel carried to our ears the whisper of a guest seated in a back row. "I wonder what she sees in *him*," the voice said. Much the same question, though more delicately phrased, has been repeatedly asked by philosophers and scientists, churchmen and psychologists, not to mention puzzled relatives and rejected suitors. Why couples choose each other remains one of the more enduring and tantalizing mysteries of human nature. What attracts two people to each other in the first place? What dynamics are at work to make them fall in love?

It is not surprising that outside observers should find it difficult to understand the specific emotional magnetisms that draw a couple together. But many men and women (perhaps most) are hard put to say exactly why they themselves were first attracted to their partners.

"I met the man who was to become my husband at a cocktail party at a friend's home. There were about thirty guests, and the conversation was typically superficial. Then this fellow started talking to me. He wasn't my type at all, physically, but after a while I found myself thinking, 'Hey, he's interesting.' He asked me to have dinner with him that night but I had another date. Impulsively I gave him my phone number and he called a few days later. He took me to a little Mexican restaurant—very casual but with good, authentic food. We sat there talking for hours. After a few more dates with him, I knew he was the man for me, but I couldn't tell you how I knew, or how it all happened. It just did."

"I was walking down the street on a summer evening and I saw this girl, a total stranger, sitting on the porch of her house reading a book." (The man is in his seventies now, and widowed, but he remembers quite clearly what happened.) "Something—*some force*—made me stop. I tipped my hat and introduced myself. She said good evening and asked if she could help me. You must realize this was fifty years ago, when people were not afraid to speak to strangers. I said, 'You don't know who I am, or anything about me, but I have a feeling you and I are going to be married.' To this day I have no idea what made me say that. I thought she would be angry or insulted, but she just laughed. 'That's impossible,' she said. 'I'm already engaged.' 'Break it off,' I replied. And do you know, three weeks later she did, and in another month we were married, just as I had said we would be."

"I've known Ellen ever since we were kids," says a forty-five-year-old man. "We were always pals; it was never anything romantic. I don't think we had what you could call a real date together until I got back from the service and went to work in her father's store. Even then our relationship was mostly platonic. But we knew each other so well, got along so compatibly, that getting married just seemed the sensible thing to do. Time has proved that it was. We are very content with each other. Most people fall in love and then marry. I guess we did it the other way around. Or maybe we *were* in love all the time and didn't know it."

According to the late Theodor Reik, an eminent psychoanalyst, two people choose each other as lovers primarily out of selfish motives. We sense something lacking in ourselves, Reik suggested, and seek the missing, better qualities in another person.[1] A bleak thought, but Erich Fromm's theory—that falling in love is an almost instinctive attempt to block out the universal fear of loneliness—is equally bleak. Yet it seems to underlie the "practical" explanation some people offer for choosing a partner:

"All my friends were married," says a thirty-three-year-old high school teacher, "my parents were having a fit that I was still single, I was tired of living alone, and the girl I was dating from time to time was a decent sort. So I just made up my mind to be in love with her, to marry her. It was time for that."

The most commonly offered explanation for choosing a partner is mutual attraction—falling in love. Yet that not only begs the question but also disregards historical fact. We have seen that only recently has love—or, for that matter, freedom of personal choice with or without love— had anything to do with the pairing off of a man and a woman.[2] Among the Incas of Peru, for example, a day was set aside each year when priests and chieftains would line up all the young men and maidens in their villages into facing rows. Then, in the name of the emperor, they would arbitrarily assign a girl to each man. Customs were even cruder in the ancient Greek city-state of Sparta. To encourage population growth and thus provide new recruits for Sparta's armies, its militaristic rulers saw to it that marriage was virtually compulsory. Bachelors were heavily penalized. They were deprived of many of the privileges of citizenship and were often publicly reviled. When all else failed the authorities would round up a random group of unwed men and women and force them into a small dark room. There each man had to pick a partner in a sort of matrimonial blind man's bluff.

A thousand years ago medieval philosophers decreed that mutual attraction followed the "natural law." It was God's will, or fate, they said, that predestined certain persons to be inevitably drawn to each other. Thus Tristan and Isolde were foredoomed to meet and drink the magic potion that made them lovers. By feudal times destiny had given way to practicality as the mainspring of matchmaking. Marriages were cold-bloodedly arranged for reasons of state and church: to foster or secure political alliances, to placate an enemy, to heal the wounds of war, to extend the temporal influence of one religion or another, to link wealthy or powerful families and assure the future by combining their influence and assets.

Even in the eighteenth century, when radical thinkers were vigorously advocating the rights of the individual, few bothered to question the authority of parents to choose a wife for their son or a husband for their daughter. When the son of the president of the *parlement* of Dijon heard rumors that he was to be betrothed to a certain mademoiselle, he asked his father if that were true. Busy with affairs of state, the father replied in effect: "Mind your own business."[3] Who would marry whom was still a matter for the family to decide; love had nothing to do with it.

While it might be quite understandable (and acceptable) for passion to be a factor in premarital or extramarital liaisons, the idea that an emotional bond was a necessary or even reasonable element in marriage was simply not considered. Indeed, many people still thought it sinful for spouses to *have* feelings of love for each other —a carry-over of early religious doctrine that held sexual longing for one's wife or husband to be the moral equivalent of adultery. Partners were expected to experience only "conjugal" affection, a sort of tepid acknowledgment of the fact that they *were* married and therefore owed each other this duty, this mere simulacrum of love. And until ten years ago dictionaries in the People's Republic of China listed the word "love" but left the definition blank. Love, it was explained, was a "decadent bourgeois silliness" not worthy of elucidation.

LOVE AS IMPULSE

A July day at a major league baseball stadium. During batting practice one of the players walks to the railing that separates the box seats from the field to chat with friends who have come to watch him play. At that moment a pretty girl in a pink sun dress approaches the group and asks the player for his autograph. Later, the young man would remember the moment this way: "I wrote my name on her ticket stub and handed it back to her. I looked at her and she looked at me. It was as if there was electricity between our eyes. Just like in the movies."

And, just like in the movies, there was a happy ending. After an exchange of letters, the player invited the girl to another game, took her to dinner afterward, eventually introduced her to his parents, and five months later married her.[4] Like the baseball player, many people describe their first meeting with the person they love in similar terms of "impulse":

"When Ted and I first met there was an instantaneous magnetism between us."

"I fell in love with Evelyn the day she came into my office. When she walked down toward the desk there was something electric about the way she moved."

"We looked at each other, and it was as if we'd been waiting for each other all these years. Wonderful feelings were zinging back and forth between us."

But is it truly possible for two persons who have never before met to sense at first look that they are meant for each other? Is it reasonable to see a stranger across a crowded room and know at a glance it's romance? The concept of love as pure impulse, an unthinking function of biological, chemical, or electrical reaction, had its brief moment of popularity at the turn of the last century. New and exciting discoveries were being made in the physical sciences, and such pseudo-scientific offshoots as early experiments with hypnotism and "animal magnetism" developed into fads. One theorist held that people fall in love because of an affinity between the chemical elements in their bodies. Another believed love was the result of deliberate search by ova and sperm: "[They] know what they lack and seek for it in another body, giving orders to their respective brains through the heart. The brain obeys without knowing why." Still others defined love as the result of a toxin in the system, a poison that maddened or diseased the brain. When this "mental degeneration" peaked, they said, a chance encounter with any person of the opposite sex could create an "impression of love" in the victim!

From that point, theories of love and attraction had nowhere to go but up. In the 1890s a Frenchman named Danville put forth the idea that each individual carried in his or her unconscious mind the image of a preferred "love type," an image created by the sights, sounds, and smells that impinged upon a person's senses at the onset of puberty, when sexual feelings were first thought to awaken. Then, Danville continued, when one meets a man or a woman who matches that latent image, it is automatically triggered into consciousness and—*voilà!*—we experience love at first sight (or sound, or odor). Through the hindsight provided by modern research techniques, we can see the possibilities of a slender thread of fact retroactively giving some support to Danville's speculations. Dr. Eugene Roberts, a Los Angeles neurochemist, has theorized that preprogrammed nerve circuits in the brain control our emotional behavior—anger, hate, fear, anxiety, love. The circuits, Roberts suggested, may be programmed by sights, sounds, odors, and other sensory information which we learn early in life to associate with specific feelings. In Roberts' view, a "command neuron" locks the circuits until incoming stimuli associated with those early emotions set them off. Theoretically, then, strangers may fall in love when each picks up the sensory signals that release their "love circuits."[5]

And when the ingenious Danville spoke of "odors" that triggered love into consciousness, could he ever have imagined that science would one day discover the existence of pheromones? Recent research has identified specific substances found in genital fluids and hormones secreted by many species of insects and mammals. These substances—called pheromones—give off a scent which plays an important part in the animals' sexual behavior. The chemical message they transmit is, in effect, a powerful mating call. The pheromones of the female gypsy moth, for instance, can attract the male moth from as far as half a mile away. In some species, both sexes produce pheromones to attract each other sexually. Human pheromones have not yet been isolated or identified, but there is increasing speculation that they do exist and that the scent they emit is an important factor in attracting men and women to each other. The chemical messengers, it is suggested, may set off electrical impulses in the brain that trigger the appropriate emotional and behavioral responses.[6]

Carl Jung, one of Freud's most famous disciples, attempted to construct an explanation of "attraction at first sight" on a genetic basis. He suggested that each man carries in his genes an "archetype," or model, of a specific female ideal. When the woman who corresponds to it appears the man cannot help but be emotionally "seized" by her. Typifying the male-dominated society of his times, Jung declared that this process did not work in reverse. A woman carries no such archetypes in her genes, he said, but must wait for Mr. Right to find her.

It is undeniably romantic to imagine that the love of one's life, the "only" woman or man in the world, is out there somewhere, unconsciously searching or patiently waiting for that climactic meeting when the secret gene patterns will interlock, the chemistry will mesh, the archetype will be "seized." The unglamorous fact, however, is that only a few experience such a revelation. And even among those who do, the passage of time often negates it. Emotions can be judged quite differently in the perspective a few years or even months can give. Surveys of college women, for instance, show that while they usually describe their feelings for a current sweetheart as "love" they describe all past attachments as "infatuations." Then too, most people fall in love with (or just plain grow to love) someone they already know, and indeed have known for quite a while: a neighbor, a classmate, a colleague at work, a friend of a friend. Studies show the odds are even that the one you love, or will love, lives within walking distance of you.[7] One researcher analyzed the geographic distribution of couples who married in a three-month period in a Midwestern city. He found that in more than half the cases both spouses lived within three quarters of a mile of each other at the time of their first date and had known each other casually for some time before they fell in love. Dr. George Armacost, for many years the president of the University of Redlands in California, would open the convocation each school year by saying to the freshman class: "Look around you in this auditorium. The person you will eventually marry is probably sitting here too."[8] Obviously, geographical nearness is a key factor in attraction. Two people must have a reasonable chance of meeting if the process is to begin at all. Moreover, the notion of a "one and only" match—whether predestined by fate, affinities, or archetypes—collapses in view of the fact that so many people marry happily more than once.

In sum, most of the early theorists of interpersonal attraction made essentially the same errors. They assumed that falling in love is a discrete act originating in a preprogrammed source point, and that the response is triggered at a specific instant, like a lightning flash. No doubt there are a handful of men and women for whom love's lightning does flash. For most others, however, love and the choice of an emotional partner is the end product of a many-faceted relationship that builds upon itself gradually and that reflects some of the basic mechanisms that govern emotional behavior.

LOVE AS LIKE AND UNLIKE

Theodor Reik once remarked that the structure and function of love could not escape the laws of psychology any more than a table could escape the law of gravity. "The question," Reik said, "is to discover just *which* laws apply."[9] But if the majority of social scientists have not chosen to do that, a few have bravely attempted to pick up the gauntlet. It is their belief, in general, that most of us tend to choose our partners less for reasons that may be tucked away in hidden crannies of the unconscious than for reasons that may be termed "environmental"— i.e., the milieu in which we grow up, the culture in which we live, and the total effect that social background exerts on personality. For example:

> Kathy and Steve first meet each other in the supermarket. Steve, standing behind Kathy at the checkout counter, observes that her cart holds many of the same food items as his does. He points to the eggplant each of them is buying. "You're the only other person I ever knew who actually liked this stuff," he says. But food preferences prove to be just one of the things the couple have in common. As they get to know each other better Kathy and Steve discover many similarities in their backgrounds. Each has grown up in a small Midwestern town, part of a large family. They like the same kind of music and poetry. They agree about religion. They share basic goals and values. It comes as no surprise to their friends when Kathy and Steve announce a few months after their first meeting that they are going to be married.

Kathy and Steve exemplify the principle that social scientists call homogamy—the attraction between persons who have much in common. Scores of sociological studies show that one is more likely to fall in love with and to marry someone who is of the same race and religion, has approximately as much intelligence and education, comes from a similar social and economic class, has roughly the same number of brothers and sisters, and has the same eye color (a result of similar ethnic background).

It may seem obvious that two people who share a substantial number of similar characteristics and values would be attracted to each other. A host of potential differences that could cause conflicts in the relationship—from preferences in food to ideas about sexual behavior, from attitudes toward religion to feelings about family—are to a large extent eliminated or at least minimized. Choosing a partner with a similar background also reduces the stresses that grow out of society's disapproval of love affairs between couples of different races, religions, disparate ages, and other "taboos."

Yet to seek to explain attraction and love by homogamy alone is a vast oversimplification. It does not take into account the chicken-and-egg effect. For as Kathy and Steve grow closer they are more likely to *want* to agree about interests and values whether or not they really do. Even if Steve originally hated eggplant he might develop a taste for it to please Kathy. Even if Kathy preferred a Neil Simon comedy to a Shakespeare tragedy she might agree to see *Macbeth* because she knows Steve enjoys the play. Thus, it is not unusual for couples to develop similar tastes and personalities *after* a few years together. Most authorities agree that homogamy does exert a substantial influence on one's choice of lover, but it is certainly not a complete answer to why couples choose each other. Not everybody places the same value on similarities. What seems most logical is to accept homogamy as a kind of weeding-out process—a way of *not* choosing someone who is far out of one's own range of values and characteristics. Indeed, a basic element of homogamy suggests, not surprisingly, that selecting a partner whose beliefs, attitudes, and feelings tend to match our own makes us more comfortable when we are with them. No doubt it also gives us less to argue about and more in common to enjoy.

But while like-minded couples may share similar backgrounds and interests, the theory of homogamy does not necessarily extend to personality traits. Some men and women—often in an unconscious effort to compensate for what they feel are lacks or shortcomings in themselves—are drawn to temperamental opposites. The idea that such psychological dovetailing is the reason why one person is strongly attracted to another was proposed some years ago by sociologist Robert Winch. He acknowledged that factors such as age, religion, education, and economic status form the basic social framework within which one is likely to meet and choose a potential partner. But the ultimate selection of a specific individual, Winch said, depends on how well their temperaments and personalities mesh. Winch concluded that we choose the one we love on the basis of "complementary needs." His theory, in essence, says that we tend to seek out a partner who has "plusses" where we have "minuses," and vice versa; someone who is competent in areas where we are not, someone whose emotional make-up completes rather than conflicts with our own.[10] For example, a young wife says:

"What first attracted me to Bob was his ability to make quick decisions. I could never do that well. I have trouble making up my mind about what I want to eat or wear, much less about important matters. So it was a relief for me to know that Bob would make these decisions for both of us."

Conversely, Bob needed to feel that in any love relationship he could be able to play the role of protector and provider. A dependent woman thus held great appeal for him. In much the same way, a man who thinks he is bright and witty and enjoys being the center of attention may well choose a shy woman who is satisfied to appreciate his cleverness. She, in turn, may be attracted to him in large part because he keeps the spotlight of attention away from her. In social situations in which she may feel awkward he will compensate for her reticence. (A recent study showed that this "witty-retiring" combination is a frequent one. Apparently there is room for only one wit in a love affair or marriage.) Complementary needs can be fulfilled on a variety of levels and across the whole spectrum of a relationship. Florence, for instance, enjoys the satisfaction she gets from cooking for someone she cares about; Harry, her fiancé, believes that being fed well is an important sign of love. He happily provides the appreciation Florence needs for her culinary efforts.

In some respects the theory of complementary needs answers the "What does she see in him?" question. For what men and women see in each other is often hidden from outsiders—and sometimes, when needs operate at deeply unconscious levels, they may even be hidden from themselves. Yet though Winch's solution may sound logical it has not proved particularly useful in predicting successful partnerships. Indeed, the "complementary" qualities many a couple believe they see in each other may not actually exist at all. A person who seems stable and confident may turn out upon closer inspection to be this way only when life is running smoothly. The first crisis often reveals a different side of his or her personality, and the partner who counted on the apparent strength feels cheated. Or a person who is openly affectionate and loving during the early stages of a relationship may become more restrained once the newness wears off. The partner who needs a good deal of overt affection now feels tricked.

If the partnership continues to function on a complementary basis, a couple will function effectively. But should circumstances or personal growth cause either partner to change—should a dependent woman want to assert her right to make some major decisions, or a dominant husband grow tired of shouldering the entire decision-making burden—the balance in the relationship may be jeopdardized. A case in point is that of Michael, a freelance writer in his early thirties. He sought counseling recently because constant battling was driving him and his wife Emily to the edge of divorce.

Michael: One of the reasons I married Emily was that she is so good at dealing with people. I am rather shy and introspective. Making friends was hard for me, and dealing with the people I had to meet in my work—editors, publishers, sources of information and research—was almost painful.

Marcia Lasswell: But your wife enjoyed the give and take of personal contact?

Michael: Very much. And I preferred to remain in the background, writing and editing the material she got through research and interviews.

M.L.: So you made a good team . . . what we'd call a symbiotic relationship, each of you doing what you can do best and both of you profiting from the result. Then what happened?

Michael: Well, we decided to have a baby, and when Emily was about six months' pregnant I began to worry about finances. I decided I had better give up free-lance work temporarily and get a job with a steady income. I went to work for a magazine as a staff writer, and after a year or so there was a big staff upheaval. Virtually overnight I was put in charge as managing editor.

M.L.: How did you feel about that? I mean in view of your shyness, were you able to handle the job?

Michael: That was the strange part. At first it was terribly difficult for me. But after a while—especially when I knew I was doing a good job on the magazine—I began to enjoy it.

M.L.: You felt in control?

Michael: That's exactly it! It was as if a whole other part of me that had been hidden suddenly came to the fore. I became more confident, sure of myself.

M.L.: And how did Emily react to this change in your personality?

Michael (grimacing): Not very well. She began trying to cut me down to size. Sometimes she'd come into the office and throw her weight around—you know, *I'm the editor's wife* sort of thing—and that really irritated me. I began to see a lot of things about Emily I hadn't noticed before, things I didn't like.

M.L.: Would it be fair to say what you had once seen as her ability to deal with people now looked to you like aggressiveness, an attempt to dominate you, to keep you in the background?

Michael: Yes . . . but I wasn't aware of it in exactly those terms for a while. When I finally confronted her with my feelings she was furious. From then on it was just argument after argument. I'd like to save my marriage, but I'm not going to go back to the kind of relationship we had before. And I don't think Emily is able to change her temperament.

Unfortunately Michael was right. Emily could not change, nor could she tolerate the changes in Michael that ended their complementarity. Ultimately the couple were divorced.

Love may not be entirely blind, but it does tend to put blinders on lovers. They seldom see each other as they really are but rather as they would ideally wish each other to be. This is not entirely the fault of poor emotional vision or the notion that wishing will make it so. There is always a certain amount of natural exaggeration (if not outright falsification) during dating or courtship. One wants to put one's best foot forward. Witness a gathering of single people who are looking for partners. She, overhearing an attractive man talking about his latest ski vacation, says, "Oh, I just *love* to ski." (She has been skiing only twice in her life but thinks she might like to do *anything* with him.) He, who has just started taking lessons himself, decides she looks interesting. He replies, "So do I. Where is your favorite place to go?" And the mystique is in the making.

Another aspect of the situation that can subtly complicate matters is that, even though one may make a fairly accurate early assessment, in the growing grip of love he or she gradually begins to assign to the beloved an increasing number of idealized virtues. Stendhal epitomized this process in one of his brilliant essays, *On Love*. Love is born, he wrote, out of admiration and hope but takes firmer shape in "a process of the mind which discovers fresh perfections in its beloved at every turn of events." Stendhal named this process "crystallization." He explained the use of the word by describing how a dead tree branch, leaf-stripped by the wind and carried into a disused salt mine, was several months later "entirely covered with glittering ice crystals" which gave it a shimmering, diamondlike coating. The ugly branch had become a thing of beauty, much as the reality of a loved one's appearance or character is idealized by the lover's imagination or self-deception. Therefore one often sees the other person not as he or she really is but as the reflected image of the "ideal lover" almost everyone dreams about. In adolescence the image is usually a stereotype: *he* must be tall and handsome, *she* must be shapely and blond. With time and maturity we add important elements: intelligence, tenderness, a sense of humor and of responsibility. The ideal varies from culture to culture. In societies in which a man needs many children to help him farm his land he envisions marrying a woman with broad hips; when a decorative partner is more of a social asset, slim and willowy figures are more desirable.

Reality seldom measures up to the ideal, of course. And

though most people try to convince themselves that the one they love really is the kind of person they dreamed of finding, the discrepancy is puzzling when it is large enough to become obvious:

David is a wealthy stockbroker who used to have a reputation as a playboy. Good-looking and much in demand by women, he would not even date a girl unless she was a beauty. "I always thought I'd marry a girl I could wear on my arm like a jewel," he said. Then he met a rather plain, serious-minded woman who intrigued him because she was not at all impressed by him. "I went out with her to break her resistance," David admitted. "Instead, she broke mine. We're going to be married next month. I know I love her, but I don't understand how it happened. I suppose I realized that beauty is usually all surface and that I really need a woman who has a mind and character."

Jerry is a television writer adept at creating characters in the scripts he turns out. "Somewhere along the way I created one for myself, a picture of the woman I wanted to marry. Of course she was going to be younger than I—but my wife is five years older! Naturally she was going to be someone with my own background and interests—but my wife is Brazilian and comes from a different cultural world. And she was going to be independent, a career woman—but my wife prefers to stay at home. I'm delighted with her—but what happened to the other me?"

LOVE AS A FAIR EXCHANGE

Ultimately most attempts to analyze why people choose the ones they love fail because the analysis is too simplistic. Few men and women fall in love for a single reason or even for a single set of reasons. In a society that permits such free choice of partners, falling in love and picking a mate are much more complicated decisions than they seem to be. A theory of attraction that has recently gained wide acceptance takes this complexity into account. It suggests that we are more likely to select a partner who offers the best "package" of practical and emotional rewards at the smallest practical and emotional cost. We tend to seek out the person, suggests psychologist Bernard I. Murstein, who represents the "fairest exchange of interpersonal assets and liabilities." In more crass terms, this "exchange" theory of attraction means that we choose an individual who appears to provide the best all-around deal we can get.[11]

One is first drawn to another person by an external stimulus: looks, voice, social or financial status, reputation. Consider John, a twenty-six-year-old architect who has always been attracted to blondes. When golden-haired Mary arrives at a party John is attending he strikes up a conversation with her at once. But Mary, he finds, lives and works in a suburban town more than an hour's drive from his city apartment. She has a built-in geographical liability as far as John is concerned and his interest in her quickly cools. For John, the emotional "reward" of Mary's blond beauty is outweighed by the time-and-distance "cost" that would be required to further their relationship. Clearly John is not a romantic or he would turn heaven and earth (or at least be willing to drive the extra miles) to be with her.

In another instance, Helen, a thirty-year-old account executive in a California brokerage firm, first met Ed on a blind date arranged by mutual friends. "When he came to pick me up my first reaction was 'How could they do this to me?' Ed was about five inches shorter than I am, almost completely bald, and overweight. I thought of making some excuse to get out of the evening but I realized that would be awfully bitchy. I figured, what the hell, it's only one time."

It was not until they met their friends at a restaurant and had ordered dinner that Helen learned Ed was a highly regarded corporation lawyer with a major firm. Moreover, a group of the town's leading businessmen were urging him to run for a seat in the state legislature. As the evening continued, Helen's attitude toward Ed changed. Her practical nature told her she shouldn't judge him too hastily by his looks. The "liabilities" of Ed's physical appearance were being balanced in her mind to some degree by the "assets" of his professional prestige, his earning ability, and his political potential. When Ed called to ask Helen for another date she accepted:

"I went out with Ed many times during the next few months," Helen said. "At first he took me to fancy places—night clubs, expensive restaurants, discos. One night I said, 'Look, you don't have to do this. I know you can afford it, but I'd just as soon be somewhere quiet, where we can talk.' He was pleased. He didn't care for all that noise and phony glitter any more than I did. And the more we talked the more we discovered how many other things we agreed about. I don't just mean things like politics or movies. We felt the same way about basic values: the kind of people we wanted for our friends, the satisfactions we wanted out of life. I had never met a man whose ideas were so close to my own. By then, too, I had grown to like how Ed looked. It all seemed to fit together."

Not surprisingly, a couple tend to develop strong positive feelings for each other when they realize they share similar values. Because Helen and Ed agreed with each other's approach to life, they reinforced each other's attitudes and aspirations. Unfortunately goals and values —key elements in a love relationship—are usually among the last things we learn about each other. Too often we react so arbitrarily to external stimuli that we do not take the time to discover more fundamental values in the other person. This excessive emphasis on externals is especially characteristic of a culture that places so much importance on appearance, dress, and status. There is a tendency quickly to rule out the physically unattractive person, the older person, the inarticulate, the unachiever as a potential partner. There is a lack of the patience and insight required to look beneath the surface and seek the more enduring and meaningful aspects of love; to say, in effect: "She's not very pretty (or, he's not handsome), but maybe if I give myself a chance to know her better I will find more important qualities that will appeal to me."

The same degree of emotional progress that Helen and Ed were making might have taken place between John and Mary if John had been willing to suspend his judgment about the rigors of the drive to Mary's home. True, his original decision—that her attractiveness did not compensate for the distance he must travel to be with her— might have been confirmed. On the other hand John might have found qualities in Mary's personality which, added to her good looks, would sufficiently appeal to him to outweigh her geographic undesirability. Where Helen's practical nature helped her to get past a first negative impression, John's practical nature overcame a first positive response.

External factors take on even more importance in what psychologists call an "open field"—an environment in which there are many people to choose among, in which relationships begin on a superficial or temporary basis, and in which one seldom has the chance or reason to get to know anyone well. In an open field an unattractive man or woman is apt to be passed over rather quickly. In a "closed field"—a small office, a classroom, a church group —not only are there fewer people but their mutual interests are likely to lead them to have contact over a sustained period of time. Under those circumstances one can come to know another person as a three-dimensional human being. In the long run the shy or awkward person may prove to be intelligent and considerate; the homely person, nurturant and understanding. A young engineer describes just such an experience:

"When Amy first came to work in my office I didn't pay much attention to her. She was rather mousy, though pleasant enough to work with. Then she and I were assigned as a team to a special design project. During the next couple of months we were thrown together quite closely and I found out how competent, thoughtful, and kind she is. More than that, Amy was the first woman who not only understood what I was trying to do professionally but had faith that I would do it. One day I realized I was in love with this girl—and suddenly she looked beautiful to me!"

Finally, exchange theory says that it is important to look at the rapport that develops between two people as a result of the satisfactions each provides the other. In short, how they "fit." If a couple continues to feel that what they can give to and get from each other approximates a fair exchange, they may decide that they are enough "in love" to live together or marry. As they spend more and more time in each other's company they become *inter*dependent. Their lives entwine in such a way that they begin to think of themselves as "we." They may feel incomplete when apart. So long as they continue this mutual dependence they have a good chance of defining themselves as "in love."

The choice of a partner, then, is basically determined by the mutual satisfactions the relationship provides. Whether lasting love develops depends on a complex combination of emotional arousal (ranging from mild to blind passion); of mutual gratification (coming from both similarities and complementarities); and, most important, whether they both define their feelings as "love."

4

THE MEASUREMENTS OF LOVE

America appears to be the only country in the
world where love is a national problem.

—Raoul de Roussy de Sales,
—*Love in America*

Love may be the only universal human experience that
has continued to defy analysis or explanation. Is love solely an emotional response? A set of behaviors? An intellectual decision about the quality of a relationship? The difficulty in making a judgment stems from a combination of
factors: the subjective nature of love, the absence of any
valid external standard by which to measure it, and the
variety of guises in which love shows itself. Is it possible
at all to dissect something at once so complex and insub-
stantial, to explore its mechanisms and explain its meaning?

Some early attempts to do this postulated a sliding scale
of levels of love. At one end was something that might be
called Love with a capital *L*, and at the other love with a
small *l*. The former is characterized as a grand passion,
exalted by history and literature in the stories of such
lovers as Hero and Leander, Heloise and Abelard, Tristan
and Isolde, Count Vronsky and Anna Karenina, Rhett
and Scarlett, King Edward VIII and Wallis Simpson. The
latter is seen as an ordinary everyday kind of love—allegedly a modest and commonplace emotion with which
lesser mortals must make do. While everyday love may
be satisfying enough for most of us, the argument runs,
only the more sublime passions are truly worthy of being
identified as the "real thing." Only Love with a capital *L*
meets the classic requirements: burning lips, vows of
eternal fealty, exquisite agonies and pleasures, and even
more exquisite frustrations or fulfillments. "The promise
of passionate experience has come to seem a promise that

we are about to live more fully, more intensely," wrote Denis de Rougement in his *Love in the Western World*. "We look upon passion as thrilling, yet passionate love is actually a misfortune."

If one takes a more discerning look at "great love" and the great lovers, a different shape emerges from the mists of sentimentality. One begins to see more pain than joy, more betrayal than devotion, more cold-bloodedness than hot-bloodedness. Little could be more cold-blooded than the behavior of the English painter and poet Dante Gabriel Rossetti. His name lives in the annals of great lovers because when his wife died he buried in her coffin the manuscripts of several of his new poems, of which there were no copies. An act of noble and impassioned feeling, to be sure. Yet a few years later, when Rossetti needed money, he exhumed his wife's body so that he could recover the manuscripts and sell them. Indeed, "great" love is more often than not characterized by actions and qualities that most of us would see as the antithesis of love. One such quality is egotism. Percy Bysshe Shelley, remembered as much for his personal romanticism as for his romantic verse, eloped with his childhood sweetheart when he was nineteen and she but sixteen. It was not long, however, before Shelley abandoned her to run away with a woman who flattered his vanity; when his child-wife drowned herself he showed no remorse. Or consider Lord Horatio Nelson, the British admiral who broke the power of the French navy. His great love, Lady Emma Hamilton, left her husband to openly become Nelson's mistress at a time when such an act cost a woman every vestige of honor and respect. Nelson did remain devoted to her, in his fashion. In a letter written while at sea he says, "I have not a thought except you and the French fleet. . . . I charge [you] to think of your Nelson's glory."

If egotism is one characteristic of Love with a capital L, a second would seem to be the need or desire to suffer. The feeling was described graphically by Thomas Otway, an English playwright, in a despairing letter to the actress Elizabeth Barry: "My love makes me mad when I am near you and . . . when I am from you. Of all miseries, love is the most intolerable, the total of all misfortunes. I cannot so much as look at you without . . . torment." The acme of mutual suffering is perhaps realized most exquisitely in the relationship of Tristan and Isolde. (And, not surprisingly, theirs ranks as probably the most famous "great love" we know.) Fated through the drinking of the magic potion to love only each other, they nevertheless denied themselves the gratification of that love out of duty and loyalty to King Mark, Tristan's lord and uncle, and Isolde's betrothed. It was the very hopelessness of their situation that fueled the ardor of their love.

Closely linked to this desire to suffer is the third key quality of Love with a capital *L*. It is the need (indeed, almost the requirement) for enormous obstacles to hinder consummation. Would Leander have been quite so taken with Hero had she lived close by and he had not been forced to swim the dangerous currents of the Hellespont each time he wanted to be with her? Would Romeo and Juliet have desired each other to the same passionate extent if their families had not forbidden them to marry? If Edward VIII had not been forced to choose between his throne and the woman he loved, would he have persisted in his course of action? It is a measure of emotional realism to be able to distinguish love from Love. For while the latter feeds on the melodrama of obstacles and separations, the former thrives on its daily, unglamorous, but far more meaningful business.

SOME NEWER—BUT STILL FLAWED— MEASUREMENTS

In recent years there have been attempts to probe the nature of love in more scientific ways. Psychologists, for example, are accustomed to classifying human reactions as either *cognitive* (having to do with thought processes), *affective* (having to do with emotional responses), or *behavioral* (having to do with actions). Accordingly, they looked for evidence that would indicate where in these categories love belongs. They devised a number of psychological and physical tests aimed at determining such things as whether or when one is "really" in love, at measuring "how much" one is in love, and discovering how one "feels" when one loves. In each case the results proved inconclusive at best, contradictory at worst.

If, for instance, love can be analyzed or measured by the way one acts toward another person, then it seems reasonable to say that behavior should be the key. After all, a researcher cannot observe an idea—what or how

someone *thinks* about love. One must study what people
say or do: how often a couple exchange loving words and
gestures, or how much time they spend gazing into each
other's eyes, or how frequently they touch, or how unselfishly they act toward each other. On that basis, presumably, a judgment can be made as to whether love is or is
not present in the relationship. But logic is seldom a hallmark of human behavior. We may act most lovingly toward someone and yet sincerely deny that we feel anything more than friendship or concern. Conversely, we
may display extreme *unloving* behavior—screaming, throw-
ing things, even striking the other person—and yet fervent-
ly declare that we love him or her.

The fact is that most people who make judgments about
love in this way (even some of the experts) do so largely
on the basis of their *own* notions of what loving behavior
is or should be. They take for granted that *they* know love
when they see it—even if the person being observed may
have quite a different idea about it. For example, such
observers may label togetherness as a sign of love when
it may actually be a sign of anxiety or insecurity. They
would have considerable trouble reaching an opinion about
a chronic adulterer who swears he or she truly loves the
spouse unless, of course, they themselves also are habitual-
ly unfaithful to the person they love.

Different problems arise when one attempts to measure
or define love on the basis of feelings. True, most people
say things like, "I feel so much love for you. . . ." But
feelings are notoriously fickle. "Today's passionate love,"
psychologist Bernard Murstein points out, "may tomorrow
be regarded as yesterday's infatuation. Indeed, the difference between love and infatuation may well be that a
successful love affair is retrospectively declared to be true
love, whereas if one is rebuffed [one] declares the relationship to have been only an infatuation."[1] The fact is that
both lovers and spouses know there are times when they
feel angry or resentful toward each other, times when they
may actually hate each other. Are they automatically no
longer in love at such moments? And do they automatically return to a state of love the instant they kiss and make
up?

For a time the techniques of biofeedback promised to
show a way out of this perplexing maze. After all, emotions like fear, anger, and anxiety had already yielded many

of their secrets to biofeedback research. Some experts thought it was similarly possible to identify feelings of love by the physical responses they produce. An emotion is more than a sentiment. It is feeling *plus* physiological change. Like every emotion, love manifests itself in bodily reactions. The poet John Donne intuited this knowledge when he wrote:

> Love's mysteries in souls do grow,
> But yet the body is his book.

Now the mechanism for testing that theory was readily at hand. Biofeedback devices can provide instrument read-outs of such telltale signs of emotion as heightened skin resistance, rapid heartbeat, a rise in body temperature and blood pressure, dilation of the pupils, even changes in brain waves. Thus it is possible to hook a person up to electrodes and measuring instruments and, by monitoring their output, deduce with considerable accuracy a great deal about his or her emotional state. Unfortunately for the love researchers, those biological read-outs prove to be much the same whether one is feeling love, fear, hate, or just generalized tension from being monitored in the first place.

Does this mean then, as many experts suspect, that emotion is all of a piece physiologically? The answer, probably, is yes. No matter what cognitive label we give to what we feel, in terms of physical responses all emotion manifests itself simply as a generalized bodily arousal. In one test, for example, experimenters instructed their subjects to recall (or to imagine) an experience which made them frightened or angry. After measuring the biofeedback read-outs and allowing time for the physical responses to return to a normal base line, the subjects were told to recall (or to imagine) an experience which made them feel loved or loving. The physiological results were virtually the same for both sets of emotions. Thus, persons who display similar physical reactions may very well be having totally different feelings.

Moreover, a couple may exhibit nearly identical biofeedback measurements when they are concentrating on feelings of love, yet their emotional reactions to those feelings may be quite incompatible—and they may disagree entirely on their cognitive definition of love. Conversely, two people may agree on what love "is" but produce wildly divergent physiological reactions to feelings of love. This disparity is more familiar when we analyze it in terms of other emotions, such as fear. Two people might respond biologically to fear in much the same way yet be frightened of different things. Conversely, an average person and a lion tamer might agree intellectually on the danger of walking into a lion's cage. Yet if the average person actually entered the cage his or her biofeedback responses would zoom; the lion tamer, knowing what he was about and concentrating on his work, would show far less intense feedback scores. The conclusion? Bodily changes can tell us that a person is experiencing *some* kind of emotion, but they cannot indicate with any reasonable degree of accuracy what that emotion is.

Interestingly, it seems that the mind can mislead the body as effectively as the body can mislead the mind. In one experiment a researcher told a group of young men that their heart rate would be recorded while they looked at photographs of nude and semi-nude women. When the experiment was over the researcher gave the men false data about the results. They were told that certain photographs caused their hearts to beat wildly, while certain others allegedly had little or no effect on them. A month later the men were asked to examine the pictures again and choose the ones that they believed excited them the most. In every case the men selected the photographs they had been told had aroused them and rejected those to which they had been told they were indifferent.[2]

The problem with most serious efforts to investigate love is that they are largely based on two unfounded premises. One is the assumption that love has the same meaning for everyone: that it consists of a single "true" feeling which then becomes the arbitrary standard for all love relationships. This leads to fruitless concerns: "Tom and Dick both say they love me, but which one *really* loves me?" Sociologist Ira Reiss has pointed out that much of the doubt people express about their love affairs "is not about whether they are experiencing *some* kind of love relationship but whether they are experiencing a *particular* type of love. . . ."[3] This one-dimensional approach is roughly as effective as asking your mother, "How will I know when I'm in love?" Her equally ineffective reply is apt to be, "Don't worry about it, you'll know when it happens."

The second flawed premise is that love can be validly measured in terms of quantity or degree, much as the device in the penny arcade rates one's "love quotient" on a scale ranging from "Blah" to "Zowie!" As a result researchers tend to ask such quantitative questions as: "How often do you feel loving?" "How long does the feeling last?" "How intense would you say the feeling is?" Seduced by the belief that love can be assessed in these ways, a person trying to decide whether he or she loves or is loved wrestles with such questions as "Does Mary love me *more* than Susan does?" "Do I love Bill *enough?*" "Have I felt this way about Jerry *long* enough to be sure it's love?" Granted, we are a ratings-minded society. But it does not make sense to assess a complex set of emotional responses in terms of duration or intensity. Does a score of, say, sixty on some numbered scale prove we do not love someone? Does a score of eighty prove we do? What is the verdict if we score seventy? Where is the cutoff line? Is there one at all? Can it possibly be the same for each of us?

We believe that love cannot be measured against some ideal standard, or weighed like potatoes, or checked for intensity like a decibel level. We are more inclined to agree with Gertrude Stein. Asked for her definition of love, the mistress of such cryptic utterances as "A rose is a rose is a rose" replied: "Love is." What's important is not how often you act loving, or how long or how much you feel loving, but, simply, how you love—what you think love is. For love is not a single indivisible concept. Rather, love has many meanings, many ways of manifesting itself, many styles. And if love means different things to different people—if each of us has a unique pattern of loving —then what counts is what you yourself think it means.

HOW TO FIND OUT WHAT YOU MEAN BY LOVE

The first attempt to identify the patterns by which men and women love was made by a Canadian sociologist, John Lee. Using the analogy of a color wheel, Lee suggested that just as there are three primary colors—red, yellow, and blue—from which all other colors are derived, so there are three primary types of love from which a larger number of combinations can be formed. Intrigued by Lee's approach, two California sociologists, Thomas E. Lasswell and Terry Hatkoff, decided to use it as a springboard for more intensive research.[4] Their goal was to develop a method for analyzing individual concepts of love. The result is the Love Scale Questionnaire on the following pages.*

An analysis of the responses of thousands of men and women who have answered the questionnaire has confirmed the existence of six basic styles of loving—six sharply divergent ways in which people define love, six contrasting patterns of behavior by which they express love. The styles were originally given descriptive Greek and Latin names; for simplicity's sake we have translated them into appropriate English equivalents. We call them: Best Friends love, Romantic love, Logical love, Game-Playing love, Unselfish love, and Possessive love.

Before we describe these styles—and before you take the Love Scale test to determine which one, or which combination of them, best reflects your own pattern—there is an important preliminary. Take five or ten minutes now to write a brief summary of what you believe love is, how you feel about it, how you think it should be expressed. It will be helpful if you think in terms of your present love relationship or, if you do not have one, in terms of your most significant past love relationship. For example, how do you normally feel about and act toward the person you love? How do you ordinarily prefer him or her to

---

* Sociological research is a complex mixture of depth interviews, pencil-and-paper testing, and statistical analysis. The Lasswell-Hatkoff Love Scale is the product of all three. To avoid the pitfall of superimposing their personal definitions of love on the responses of subjects, the sociologists first collected thousands of statements from interviewees and quotations from literature which reflected opinions about and attitudes toward love. A panel of experts then sorted these statements and quotations into categories of love styles that seemed distinct from one another. Using techniques of statistical analysis, fifty statements were ultimately selected as being most representative of these categories. To date this Love Scale has been tested on thousands of men and women of various racial, ethnic, religious, educational, and age groups. It is now used as a research tool in many universities and for diagnostic purposes by marriage and family therapists.

feel about and act toward you? In essence, what does "being in love" mean to you? For your guidance here is a typical summary:

> When I am in love, I feel very comfortable. I want to spend as much time as I can with my lover but I don't like to feel possessed. I try to do thoughtful things to show my love. He likes to be touched a lot more than I do so I make a point of being affectionate as often as I comfortably can. I buy him little gifts and fix his favorite dishes. I'll run an errand or do a task for him that I know he's dreading. I want him to be thoughtful of me too. I like gifts and attention. I want him to let everyone know I'm his special love. Being in love means that he is all I need. I'd rather be with him than anyone else. He is my best friend. We confide in each other and share the good and bad. I like some romance too, but being comfortable is the main ingredient.

Here is another, quite different summary statement:

> I feel exhilarated when I am in love. Every sense seems sharper, every feeling more intense. I consider myself very committed to the person I love, and I expect her to be equally committed to me. At the same time, though, I must admit that I still feel attracted to other women and wish I could have more than one lover at a time. I want the person I love to be totally interested in what I am doing. I want her to be openly affectionate, sexually provocative, and sexually involved. I am that way with her. I have a tendency to be jealous, but I've learned jealousy is counterproductive to love, so I fight it down. Another tendency I try to combat is a need to be in control of the woman I love—to know what she thinks and feels all the time, to know what she is doing, where she is going when she isn't with me. All in all I think being in love is when life is most interesting and exciting. I guess I enjoy the challenge, no matter how the relationship works out in the long run. My feeling is, "It's better to have loved and lost than never to have loved at all."

Remember, in order to derive the most benefit from the results of the questionnarie itself it is important that you write your personal statement before going on. It will be useful later to validate or to counterpoint your replies to the Love Scale items.

You are now ready to answer the fifty questions on the Love Scale. Each one is to be answered "true" or "false." Your responses will indicate the key characteristics of your beliefs, feelings, memories, and information about love, and will reveal which style of love is uniquely yours. Answer the questions in consecutive order and do not skip or omit any of them. Even if you feel that you cannot give a categorical "true" or "false" reply to any specific question, choose the answer you believe best reflects your ideas and attitudes most of the time. Remember, there is no provision for such in-between responses as "sometimes," "occasionally," or "maybe."

As with the summary you have written, answer these questions in terms of your current or your most significant love relationship. Finally, if you and your partner are both answering the questionnaire, do so separately. Do not discuss either the questions or your potential answers with each other in advance, and do not attempt to influence each other's responses. Of course, no psychological test or sociological study can presume to offer a definitive verdict about any aspect of human nautre, especially one so abstruse as love. It must be emphasized, therefore, that an individual score recorded on the Love Scale is not to be taken as an infallible result. It is, however, highly indicative of one's main attitudes and preferences.

THE LOVE SCALE QUESTIONNAIRE

1. I believe that "love at first sight" is possible.
2. I did not realize that I was in love until I actually had been for some time.
3. When things aren't going right for us, my stomach gets upset.
4. From a practical point of view, I must consider what a person is going to become in life before I commit myself to loving him/her.
5. You cannot have love unless you have first had *caring* for a while.
6. It's always a good idea to keep your lover a little uncertain about how committed you are to him/her.

7. The first time we kissed or rubbed cheeks, I felt a definite genital response (lubrication, erection).

8. I still have good friendships with almost everyone with whom I have ever been involved in a love relationship.

9. It makes good sense to plan your life carefully before you choose a lover.

10. When my love affairs break up I get so depressed that I have even thought of suicide.

11. Sometimes I get so excited about being in love that I can't sleep.

12. I try to use my own strength to help my lover through difficult times, even when he/she is behaving foolishly.

13. I would rather suffer myself than let my lover suffer.

14. Part of the fun of being in love is testing one's skill at keeping it going and getting what one wants from it at the same time.

15. As far as my lover goes, what he/she doesn't know about me won't hurt him/her.

16. It is best to love someone with a similar background.

17. We kissed each other soon after we met because we both wanted to.

18. When my lover doesn't pay attention to me I feel sick all over.

19. I cannot be happy unless I place my lover's happiness before my own.

20. Usually the first thing that attracts my attention to a person is his/her pleasing physical appearance.

21. The best kind of love grows out of a long friendship.

22. When I am in love I have trouble concentrating on anything else.

23. At the first touch of his/her hand I knew that love was a real possibility.

24. When I break up with someone I go out of my way to see that he/she is okay.

25. I cannot relax if I suspect that he/she is with someone else.

26. I have at least once had to plan carefully to keep two of my lovers from finding out about each other.

27. I can get over love affairs pretty easily and quickly.

28. A main consideration in choosing a lover is how he/she reflects on my family.

29. The best part of love is living together, building a home together, and rearing children together.
30. I am usually willing to sacrifice my own wishes to let my lover achieve his/hers.
31. A main consideration in choosing a partner is whether or not he/she will be a good parent.
32. Kissing, cuddling, and sex shouldn't be rushed. They will happen naturally when one's intimacy has grown enough.
33. I enjoy flirting with attractive people.
34. My lover would get upset if he/she knew some of the things I've done with other people.
35. Before I ever fell in love I had a pretty clear physical picture of what my true love would be like.
36. If my lover had a baby by someone else I would want to raise it, love it, and care for it as if it were my own.
37. It is hard to say exactly when we fell in love.
38. I couldn't truly love anyone I would not be willing to marry.
39. Even though I don't want to be jealous I can't help it when my lover pays attention to someone else.
40. I would rather break up with my lover than to stand in his/her way.
41. I like the idea of having the same kinds of clothes, hats, plants, bicycles, cars, etc., as my lover does.
42. I wouldn't date anyone that I wouldn't want to fall in love with.
43. At least once when I thought a love affair was all over, I saw him/her again and the old feelings came surging back.
44. Whatever I own is my lover's to use as he/she chooses.
45. If my lover ignores me for a while I sometimes do really stupid things to try to get his/her attention back.
46. It would be fun to see whether I can get someone to go out with me even if I didn't want to get involved with that person.
47. A main consideration in choosing a partner is how he/she will reflect on one's career.
48. When my lover doesn't see me or call for a while, I assume he/she has a good reason.

49. Before getting very involved with anyone I try to figure out how compatible his/her hereditary background is with mine in case we ever have children.

50. The best love relationships are the ones that last the longest.

HOW TO SCORE YOUR LOVE SCALE ANSWERS

To score your responses to the questionnaire, the only answers that need to be considered are the "true" responses. The table below shows a heading for each style of love:

BEST FRIENDS	UNSELFISH	LOGICAL	POSSESSIVE	ROMANTIC	GAME PLAYING
2.	12.	4.	3.	1.	6.
5.	13.	9.	10.	7.	14.
8.	19.	16.	11.	17.	15.
21.	24.	28.	18.	20.	26.
29.	30.	31.	22.	23.	27.
32.	36.	38.	25.	35.	33.
37.	40.	42.	39.	41.	34.
50.	44.	47.	43.		46.
	48.	49.	45.		
Total——	Total——	Total——	Total——	Total——	Total——

Put a check by the number of each question that you answered "true." Total the number of check marks in each column. Your test profile will probably show some "true" answers in all the classifications, but with peak scores in two or three of them. For example, you may have answered "true" to four questions of the eight in the Best Friends category and to six questions of the nine in the Logical one. We could then reasonably assume that you are a person who is quite practical in terms of whom you can love and how you love them, but that you also want to make the person you love your closest friend.

Here is another illustration: Say you have answered "true" to four questions of the nine in the Unselfish category and to four of the seven in the Romantic group. It is reasonable to interpret this to mean that you feel a strong physical attraction to a partner at the outset of a relationship; and that you believe that if your love is a true one it will overcome every obstacle, even to the point of giving each other up if that will make you both happier.

Some of you may have scored high (70 per cent or more "true" answers) in several or even all of the categories. This does not necessarily mean your definitions of love are confused. It is more apt to be a measure of your tendency to agree with a statement even though for you it may be only partially or occasionally true. On the other hand, some of you may have moderate to low scores (50 per cent or fewer "true" answers on all of the six scales). This does not mean that you are not a loving person or that your ideas about the meaning of love are hopelessly muddled. What it does mean, most likely, is that you are inclined to be analytical and cautious about your emotional responses and behavior, as well as about deciding how to answer questionnaires such as this one. Thus, if there is any doubt at all in your mind about a statement or your reaction to it, you have probably answered "false." Nevertheless, low scores are just as important a measure of your attitude as high scores are. If you have both some low and some high scores, the low scores can be equally revealing since they tend to reflect what you *do not* believe love to be.

5

THE SIX BASIC STYLES

How do I love thee? Let me count the ways.
—Elizabeth Barrett Browning, *Sonnets
from the Portuguese*

As your Love Scale score probably indicates, most people conceive of love as a combination of styles—perhaps Best Friends with a touch of the Romantic, or Romantic with a touch of Game Playing. We'll be discussing the most frequently encountered mixtures of styles later. But it is important first to understand the characteristics of what we might call each "pure" style of love. They are listed in this chapter alphabetically, to underline the fact that they do not occur or develop in any specific sequence. Nor is there any hierarchy of values so far as love styles are concerned. One is not necessarily more or less mature than another, nor do we necessarily grow out of one style and into another as we move through life.

BEST FRIENDS LOVE

When Jennifer and Gary told their families they were going to be married the news was a pleasant surprise to everyone. "We knew they were close," said Jennifer's mother. "After all, our families have lived on the same block for years and the children went through school together. Jenny was almost always Gary's 'date' when there was a dance or party. But we never dreamed they would fall in love." For that matter, neither did Jennifer nor Gary. "Actually," the young woman said, "it's not as if we *fell* in love at all. It's more like we're comfortable with each other—we know each other's good qualities and we're used to each other's faults. We have a really warm and easy relationship, so why bother to search for anyone else?"

When another couple, Chuck and Sally, announced their

engagement their friends were astonished. "I knew they
worked together in the same law firm for five years," one
said, "but there was never the slightest hint of anything
between them beyond their professional relationship."
Chuck was rather surprised himself. "I can't pinpoint exactly what prompted me to propose. One day I simply
realized I was in love with Sally because we have so much
in common, and because we get along so well when we're
together." In effect, Chuck discovered he had *been* in
love with Sally a long time before he realized what he was
feeling.

Both of these couples are examples of the love style we
call "Best Friends"—a comfortable intimacy that develops
out of close association and identity of interests over a
substantial period of time. For persons in whom this style
predominates, love grows through companionship, rapport,
mutual sharing and dependency, gradual self-revelation.
There is seldom any assumption at the outset of the relationship that it will flower into love or marriage. Friendly
lovers find it hard to conceive of becoming emotionally
involved with someone they do not know well. They rarely fantasize about other potential lovers or hope for a
Prince or Princess Charming to appear. Even if this
thought *should* occur to them, they would probably want
to share it with the partner. After all, the reasoning would
run, isn't that what a best friend is for? Such persons tend
to speak of their kind of love as 'mature" compared to
some other styles which they are likely to see as infatuation or sentimentality.

The "pure" Best Friend lover is seldom passionate or
romantic. He or she will be loving in a thoughtful, warm,
companionable way. It is not that a person with this love
style deliberately avoids intense emotions. Rather, intensity of feeling is foreign to his or her nature. Pierre
Proudhon, a social philosopher, might have been describing this style when he wrote about a love "without fever,
tumult or folly." This is not to say that Best Friend lovers
never become upset or argue with a partner. But when
there is disagreement or even outright conflict, the matter
is usually discussed rationally and resolved amicably—a
consummation made possible by the reservoir of warmth
and mutual affection on which a Best Friend lover can
draw. To the friendly lover, an argument is not cause for
concern that love is no longer present. Nor is it any

reason for the relationship to be damaged or ended. Once a Best Friend lover permits emotional intimacy to develop, he or she considers it to be a permanent commitment.

Typically, a person with this love style is the product of an emotionally secure and close-knit family. He or she has usually been able to count on parents and siblings for companionship, warmth, support. Indeed, in many respects Best Friends love resembles a good sibling relationship. Some disagreements are expected and tolerated, temporary separations are normal; neither event is looked upon as a threat to closeness. And since in such families there tends to be enough love for all to share, the friendly lover seldom feels jealous of a partner. As a result, brief (or even lengthy) absences arouse no anxiety. (This may explain why a Best Friend lover can remain happily loyal even though a partner may be away for long periods on business or military service.) Friendly lovers frequently exchange calls or letters during absences, in large part because they have so much to share with each other. When someone is your best friend it is natural to want him or her to know what you have been doing and to want to know what he or she has experienced.

The divorce rate for Best Friends couples is very low. But if such a relationship should break up a Best Friend lover will most likely want to remain close to the former partner. He or she would find it inconceivable, says John Lee, "that two people who had once loved each other could become enemies simply because they had ceased to be lovers." On occasion, such couples continue to care about each other even after one or both persons have formed a new relationship. For example, one woman still asks her ex-husband to dinner once or twice a month; and he stocks her freezer with game from his hunting trips. "I will always be his friend," she said, "just as I know I can always count on him in an emergency." As we shall see, this sort of relationship would be virtually impossible in a different love style. But being a Best Friend lover implies having stable and reasonable emotional responses.

GAME-PLAYING LOVE

To the Game-Playing lover an emotional relationship is a challenge to be enjoyed, a contest to be won. The more experienced one grows at the game the more skilled one's moves can be, and often a wide range of strategies and tactics are developed to keep the game interesting. The rules were formulated two thousand years ago when Ovid wrote *The Art of Love*. In it he coined the phrase *amor ludens*—love as a game. The object of the game is to play amiably at love, to encourage intimacy yet to hold it at arm's length. This style's motto might well be, "It isn't whether you win or lose, it's how you play the game."

Commitment is virtually anathema to the Game-Playing lover, either on one's own part or that of one's partner. The other person must always be kept emotionally off balance, and the Game Player's affections are never to be taken for granted. Indeed, it is not unusual for a person who employs this style to have two or more love partners simultaneously. He or she believes in having many affairs before settling down to one, and may periodically have an affair after settling down. In an emergency he or she may even create a fictional "lover" to discourage a real one's hopes:

> "I really liked Carol," a Game-Playing man told us recently, "but she knew it and began pressuring me to be more serious about our relationship. She also knew I had broken off with another woman and had not been seeing anyone else but her. I got the idea of *making up* a new lover. I called her Pandora. I mean Carol *had* to believe she was real. Would anyone fake a story like that and have the nerve to give the girl a phony-sounding name like Pandora? I began dropping remarks about how 'Pan and I saw that movie the other night.' I even left a slip of paper near the phone with Pandora's name and 'telephone number' on it. After a while Carol got the message and stopped assuming we were going to be a permanent twosome."

Game-Playing lovers have many such artifices. For example, they avoid making long-range plans with partners. Dates are usually arranged on a spur-of-the-moment basis. They are careful, too, not to go out with the same person too often; that might lead him or her to believe there was some prospect of stability—some emotional future—for the relationship. And as another "distancing" strategy, Game-Playing lovers choose not to reveal their innermost thoughts and feelings; nor do they want such revelations from a partner.

Much of this kind of love style is found prior to marriage when a one-to-one commitment is not required or expected. But even after they are engaged or wed, Game Players find ways to continue the game. Indeed, some of them contrive real or fancied "risk" situations to give emotional spice to a relationship that might otherwise grow boring. For it is the challenge, above all, that motivates them. One married man who scored high on Game Playing told us: "The one thing I can't stand is when my wife clings to me emotionally. I love her the most after we've had a fight, or when I see her flirting with another man. I couldn't love a woman who isn't provocative." Rather than feeling jealous when someone pays romantic attention to his wife, this man sees it as a form of flattery—a compliment to his taste and skill in the game of love.

Obviously, men and women who play at love have both charming and infuriating qualities. They are usually self-sufficient, making few demands on the other person and preferring not to have demands made on them. They also tend to be amusing, quick-witted, self-confident. On the other hand, by treating an emotional relationship as a game and not letting the other person know it, these lovers reveal their essential self-centeredness and their willingness to exploit a partner's feelings. A woman may deliberately set out to see how much she can get from a man while committing herself to him as little as possible in return. A man may try to see how much he can get from a woman for a minimum of emotional investment on his part. The pleasure seems to come as much from confirming that one has played the game expertly as from actually "winning" it.

The charge often is made that Game-Playing love is not truly love at all, that it is hedonism at best and promiscuity at worst. But the true Game-Playing lover believes in playing fair. When John Lee interviewed a number of men and women Game Players he found that most of them were careful not to go to such lengths that the other person would be hurt. Yet Game-Playing love *can* be devastating (especially in marriage) unless both partners have this same style and are well matched at the game. Indeed, most people who fall into this category recognize the need for alternative approaches should Game Playing become too emotionally damaging. Others who cannot shift styles as easily often transfer their need for challenge and variety from the arena of love to the arena of work.

LOGICAL LOVE

"It is impossible to love and be wise," wrote Francis Bacon. "People who are sensible about love are incapable of it." But the Logical lover does not agree. He or she concentrates on the practical values that may be found in a relationship. This style has been called love with a shopping list. "I could never love anyone who didn't meet my requirements for a husband and father (or wife and mother)," is a typical attitude. Moreover, Logical lovers are quite realistic. They usually know exactly what kind of partner they want or need and are willing to wait for the person who comes closest to meeting most (but not necessarily all) of their specifications. And they are keenly aware of the alternatives that may be available.

It is not uncommon for a lover of this pragmatic bent to avoid any relationship, even the most casual, unless he or she thinks there is a good chance of its becoming permanent. "Why should I waste my time?" one man asked. "I know what I want in a lover or a wife, and I don't see why I should get involved with anyone who doesn't meet my needs." From his point of view, this man was making good sense. He not only knew what he required of a partner in the way of appearance, education, family background, and personality; he also was keenly aware of what he had to offer in terms of assets and liabilities. "I'm neither wealthy nor handsome," he said, "so I cannot expect a glamorous beauty to be interested in me. But I am hard-working, dependable, and stable. A women who appreciates those qualities and who is able to reciprocate them certainly ought to be attracted to me." In short, Logical lovers, wittingly or unwittingly, practice the theory of fair exchange. They estimate their "market value" and seek to make the best possible "deal" in a love relationship.

In one sense Logical love is an updated version of the traditional "arranged" matchmaking of earlier times. (Today computer-match dating services often cater to this practical approach.) The modern Logical lover may believe that romance does have some place in love; but he or she feels more strongly that love should be an outgrowth of—and in turn serve to deepen—a couple's practical compatibility. It is not unusual for a Logical lover to avoid or postpone a love relationship until he or she has, for example, saved a certain amount of money, been promoted to a specific job, finished graduate school, or successfully ended psychotherapy.

Some Logical lovers go to even greater lengths. For instance, a man who had three children in a previous marriage, and who does not want any more, has not allowed himself to become emotionally involved with any woman who has or wants children. In another case a woman whose first marriage foundered because of continued interference from in-laws makes it a rule, early on in any new relationship, to meet and "check out" close relatives of any man to whom she feels attracted. Similarly, a Logical lover would not consider it strange to make sure, before marriage, that his or her Rh factor was compatible with the other person's, or to seek genetic counseling to assess the risk of hereditary defects. None of this is to say that a person with this love style is cynical or cold-hearted. It is simply that reason predominates over feeling. But once he or she is satisfied that a sensible choice has been made, warmer emotions take over.

Pragmatic lovers consider themselves in love so long as the relationship is perceived as a fair exchange. If matters turn out to be not what they seemed, or if a partner shows a tendency toward a significant change, Logical love calls for a two-step response. First, an effort is made to help the partner fulfill his or her original potential. "I married Jim in our first year of law school," one young woman said, "because I thought we would make an excellent working team. But once we were married he began to worry about finances. When Jim said he was going to drop out of law school to take a high-paying job, I realized that would have ruined all my plans, so *I* left school instead, and went to work until he graduated. As soon as Jim was hired by a law firm I returned to school and got my degree. Now we are working together, just as I planned." If such efforts fail, then a Logical love style dictates putting an end to the relationship. "I couldn't continue to respect him," a woman said of her former fiancé. "We had agreed that when I finished college he would join me in going to graduate school. We applied and were accepted. We moved to the university but he never started in the program. There were always excuses. Finally I decided he didn't want to complete with me. I realized I couldn't love someone who was afraid I'd do a better job, so I broke our engagement."

Sometimes the pragmatic approach dictates more than one relationship at a time. Even though the "true" loved one meets the basic requirements, other lovers may be taken, temporarily and clandestinely, for sexual excitement, intellectual stimulation, or to meet other needs. Psychoanalyst Robert Seidenberg tells of a husband, a prominent man in his small home town, who was suspected of having an adulterous affair because he was seen visiting a woman friend several evenings each week. But sex had nothing to do with it. The man enjoyed reading poetry, and since his wife was not interested in poetry he took the practical step of finding someone who was.[1] Of course, in the event of a conflict between the primary and secondary relationships, the Logical lover will almost invariably renounce the latter. Strange as this pattern may seem to most Americans, it is fairly common elsewhere in the world. Statesmen, industrialists, the wealthy, and the creative often maintain one relationship for family stability and public consumption and a second for personal pleasure. What, after all, could be more logical?

Not surprisingly, a pragmatic love style demands patience. Patience to find the satisfactory partner in the first place; patience to work out problems; and even patience —if love dies—to wait to end the relationship at a reasonable and logical time. Pragmatic lovers adopt the same attitude toward the breakdown of a partnership as they do to its formation. A spouse may plan years ahead for a divorce, waiting until the couple's children have grown or until the family's financial situation makes divorce affordable. A lover may wait to break off an affair until he or she feels the other person is emotionally strong enough to handle the rejection.

POSSESSIVE LOVE

The Possessive lover represents perhaps the most unfulfilling and disturbing style. Alternating between peaks of excitement and depths of despair, capable of shifting in an eyeblink from intense devotion to intense jealousy or even to antipathy, he or she is consumed by the need to possess the beloved totally—and simultaneously to *be* possessed by the other person. The fear of loss or rejection is omnipresent. Despite this bleak picture, this pattern is usually considered one of the most common definitions of being in love.

In ancient times a Possessive lover was believed cursed by the gods, literally the victim of a divine sort of madness. Today we understand that this frantic need to feel—to *know*—that one is loved stems largely from emotional insecurity. There is, in the Possessive love style, a constant search for reassurance: "Tell me that you love me!" Separations—whether brief or lengthy, voluntary or involuntary, even if forced by illness or by business or family obligations—may be considered virtual betrayals: "How can you be willing to leave me if you really love me?" Promises are extracted: "I want you to call me every day!" If the partner is late for a date or, worse yet, is forced to break one, the Possessive lover sees it not as an accident or an unhappy occurrence but as a breach of trust. Every incident is personalized.

At the root of Possessive love are two seemingly contradictory emotional factors. On the one hand, as we have seen, such lovers are enormously dependent. At the outset of a love affair they may be too excited to sleep, to eat, to think clearly. Unable to control their intense reactions, they often feel helplessly at the mercy of the beloved. Thus the protagonist of Lawrence Durrell's novel *Justine* says of the woman to whom he is attracted: "But what made me afraid was that after quite a short time I found to my horror that I could not live without her . . . I had fallen in love. The very thought filled me with an inexplicable despair . . ."

Yet at the same time such lovers are demanding, often to the point where they have no compunction about placing great emotional burdens on the other person. Supersensitive, the Possessive lover is constantly alert for the slightest sign that the partner's affection may be slackening. If such a sign is detected, or even imagined, the anxiety-ridden lover demands immediate reassurance. Unlike the Game-Playing lover, he or she is inordinately jealous if a partner pays attention to anyone else. Possessives require exclusiveness in a relationship:

"When I finally forced myself to admit exactly what Ron was trying to do to me," says a young woman who recently broke off her relationship with such a lover, "I was horrified that I'd let him get away with it for so long. He had managed to cut me off, one by one, from almost all my friends. He resented it every time I visited or talked on the phone with my family. He convinced me to resign from a choral group, saying that it kept me away from him too many nights. Every time I'd try to protest he'd say he wanted us to be everything to each other, that there was no room for outsiders."

Like the Game-Playing lover, the Possessive lover is—or tries to be—manipulative. But because his or her emotions take control of logical thinking, the plans may backfire. For example, Mary may tell John she thinks they should not see each other for a week or two so they can think objectively about their relationship. But chances are that after only a day or so of being separated Mary will panic at the idea of being apart from John, or at the thought that he may be seeing another woman. John, for his part, may seek to manipulate Mary via the telephone ploy. Forcing himself *not* to make his customary nightly call, he decides to see how long Mary will wait before calling *him*. But when the phone does not ring soon, John's anxiety and jealousy get the better of his will power. He telephones Mary to make sure she is home and not out with someone else.

When affairs with Possessive lovers break up the ending is usually angry and bitter. Unlike the Best Friend, the Possessive lover finds it almost impossible to see his or her former partner again or to retain any shred of concern or affection for him or her. It is the fact of the loss itself that gnaws, and the Possessive lover tends to pick over a dead affair in an anguished effort to find out what went wrong. Still, the Possessive lover is perhaps more to be pitied than condemned. "He knows his possessiveness and jealousy are self-defeating, but he cannot help himself," says John Lee. In Somerset Maugham's *Of Human Bondage* the hero, Philip, is in love this way with Mildred, an unattractive, selfish, whining, and thoroughly unrewarding girl. Philip comes to despise himself for loving her but is unable to stop himself. He, like so many others who love in this style, is a victim of a virtual addiction to the other person. Psychologist Stanton Peele observed that when one's "attachment to . . . another person is such as to lessen his appreciation of and ability to deal with other things in his environment, or in himself, [and one becomes] increasingly dependent on that experience as his only source of gratification,"[2] a literal love addiction exists. Peele equates the use of another individual with the use of drugs as a way of escaping from one's own anxiety or low self-esteem. A dramatic case of possibly mutual addiction occurred some years ago when a young attorney, rebuffed by a woman he passionately desired, hired a thug to throw lye in the woman's face so that no other man would want her. The woman's face was badly disfigured. The attorney was sentenced to fifteen years in prison. During much of that time he continued to write to the woman, and when he was finally released they got married.

It is easy to give Possessive love a bad name, to concentrate on its unpleasant characteristics. Nevertheless, it has been our experience that many perfectly adequate and emotionally healthy men and women evidence this style of love to some degree. Often passionate in all that they do, loving can be no exception. They prefer intense togetherness but do not go to pieces over temporary separations. They see jealousy as a natural part of being in love, and may even declare that anyone who does not feel jealous now and then cannot possibly feel love, either.

ROMANTIC LOVE

Cupid's arrow piercing the heart and instantaneously awakening passionate devotion—no other image so accurately delineates this style. The Romantic lover is often as much in love with love itself as with the beloved. Love at first sight is not only possible but almost a necessity: it is as if he or she has been waiting for the arrow to strike home. "Don't you think I was made for you?" Zelda Fitzgerald asked F. Scott Fitzgerald shortly after they met. "I feel like you had me ordered—and I was delivered to you."[3] Once such a meeting occurs, the Romantic lover cannot bear to be separated from the object of his or her affections. So Napoleon Bonaparte (whose complex love style was heavily laced with romanticism) wrote from his battle headquarters in Nice to Josephine:

I have not spent a day without loving you; I have not spent a night without embracing you; I have not so much as drunk a single cup of tea without cursing the pride and ambition which force me to remain separated from the moving spirit of my life. In the midst of my duties . . . my beloved Josephine stands alone in my heart, occupies my mind, fills my thoughts. If I am moving away from you with the speed of the Rhone torrent, it is only that I may see you again more quickly. If I rise to work in the middle of the night, it is because this may hasten by a matter of days the arrival of my sweet love.

The typical Romantic lover seeks a total emotional relationship with a partner. Moreover, he or she expects it to provide a constant series of emotional peaks. The fires of this love style are fueled in large part by a powerful sense of physical attraction. As the eighteenth-century English essayist Richard Steele wrote to his fiancée, Mary Scurlock: "Madam, it is the hardest thing in the world to be in love and yet attend to business. . . . A gentleman asked me this morning, 'What news from Lisbon?' and I answered, 'She is exquisitely handsome.' "[4] Romantics place much importance on appearance. They dwell in both conversation and imagination on a lover's physical features. Many Romantics have a conscious or unconscious ideal of beauty, a sensual anticipation and memory of another's body. "I can still remember exactly the way he looked the first time I saw him," one woman says. "It was just the way I dreamed my ideal lover would look." These first meetings are often etched into the Romantic's memory. So Anne Morrow writes of her first sight of Charles Lindbergh:

I saw standing against the great stone pillar . . . a tall boy in evening dress . . . so much slimmer, so much taller, so much more poised than I had expected. A very refined face . . . a firm mouth, clear, straight blue eyes, fair hair, and nice color.[5]

The Romantic lover will not only remember how the beloved looked but will cling to a host of other sentimental details: what the weather was like on the day they met, how it felt the first time they touched, what the other person said, did, even what he or she wore. The composer Robert Schumann writing to his fiancée, Clara Wieck, illustrates this:

> Once you were in a black dress, going to the theatre. . . . I know you will not have forgotten; it is vivid with me. . . . And yet another time, as you were putting on your hat after a concert, our eyes happened to meet, and yours were full of the old unchanging love. I picture you in all sorts of ways, as I have seen you since.

But memory alone is not enough for the true Romantics. They want to know everything about the partner—all of his or her experiences, joys, sorrows, past loves. They also want to open all of themselves to the partner—to reveal their innermost thoughts, secrets, problems, and hopes. It is as if every scrap of information that is shared forges the bonds of love more firmly. Then too, Romantic lovers often use this information to discover new ways to please the one they love with words, gifts, even imaginative sexual techniques. Finally, they seek to cement the relationship by creating identifying links between themselves and the beloved. Romantic lovers will put their initials on a present given to the partner, or wear matching clothes, or even order the same foods when dining together. Birthdays and anniversaries, of course, are never forgotten.

Once they have found each other, two Romantic lovers are likely to be in each other's arms quickly. Each has found the person he or she has been waiting for, the person who will share his or her love forever. There is a great urgency to merge physically as well as emotionally. Obviously the intensity of this initial attraction and passion cannot be maintained indefinitely at the same high level. When it begins to taper off, the Romantic lover must either substitute fantasies for realities or confront the growing evidence that the other person is not, after all, perfect. But for those Romantic lovers who manage to survive this transition (and many do), the original excitement continues to smolder and is frequently rekindled. "We've been married twenty years," a man declares, "and sometimes when I catch sight of my wife unexpectedly I still find myself thinking how beautiful she is." A woman says: "When I first see my husband again after he has been away on a business trip I feel all fluttery inside. There's no question but that he can still excite me just as he did when we first met." Sometimes these feelings are not objectively true, but it is important to Romantic lovers to *believe* they are. In any event, this attitude often helps Romantics to tolerate or ignore the daily minor irritations that occur when two people live together intimately.

It may seem that a person whose love style is Romantic suffers from unconscious doubts about his or her qualities as a lover, and uses these techniques and devices as a desperate attempt to compensate, to "guarantee" closeness. Actually, however, a person must have a good deal of self-assurance to be a true Romantic. One must be willing and able to reveal oneself completely, to commit oneself totally, to risk emotional lows as well as highs, and, finally, to survive without despair if one's love is rejected. A Romantic does not demand love, as some with different love styles do, but is confidently ready to grasp it when it appears.

UNSELFISH LOVE

Unselfish love is unconditionally caring and nurturing, giving and forgiving, and, at its highest level, self-sacrificing. Generations of high school students will remember the scene in Dickens' *Tale of Two Cities* in which Sydney Carton goes willingly to the guillotine in place of Charles Darnay. Both men loved Lucie Manette, but Carton knew that she cared more for Darnay than for him. To Carton, giving up his own life for the sake of Lucie's happiness was "a far, far better thing . . . than I have ever done." It is characteristic of this love style that one has no sense of martyrdom, no feeling of being put upon. Rather, it rests upon the genuine belief that true love is better expressed in giving than in receiving; in caring more about the loved one's welfare and happiness than about one's own; in postponing or giving up one's own hopes and goals to help a partner reach his or hers. But Unselfish love does not always require the melodramatic gesture of a Sydney Carton. This note, scribbled on scratch paper, which a young woman received from a man whose love she could not return is just as nobly altruistic:

> Though I know, of course, that it will hurt me, more than anything, I hope that you will find that special

someone who can fill that space inside you that needs so desperately to be filled—even more desperately than my need for you. I will always care about you deeply, but I guess I can prove that best by wishing that you will find the right man to share your tears and laughter.

Unselfish love can still be compassionate even when a partner causes great emotional pain. Typically, it takes the attitude that the other person is acting out of ignorance or innocent error, or is the victim of external forces he or she cannot control. One man, for example, wholeheartedly adopted the baby his wife had by a lover who deserted her when he learned she was pregnant. "I love her," the husband explained simply. A woman remained loyal to the man who had compulsively gambled away their savings and their home. "He couldn't help himself," she said. "You don't stop loving a man just because he has a problem." Another wife, whose husband divorced her after sixteen years of marriage to be with a younger woman, refused to ask for alimony or to set vindictive conditions on his child-visitation rights. "Even though he hurt me, I cannot hurt him," she said. The truly Unselfish lover is uncomplainingly supportive, willing to wait indefinitely for the beloved, willing to tolerate indefinitely the most hurtful or destructive behavior. Love ends only when the Unselfish lover believes he or she no longer fulfills the other person's needs.

This style of love is sometimes called "agapic." Derived from the Greek, the word reflects the Christian ideal of love said to flow from God—a love offered with no thought of return. In his letter to the Corinthians, St. Paul called love a duty to care about others, whether such caring is deserved or not. In a sense, it may be said that men and women whose style of love this is never actually "fall in love." Rather, they seem to have a reservoir of loving-kindness which is always available and which they readily offer when the opportunity arises. Unselfish lovers are ruled less by their own emotional needs than by the needs of others.

Though it is frequently described and celebrated in fiction, drama, and poetry, Unselfish love occurs less often in real life. Not many people have the emotional fortitude to be so giving. Even if they do, however, their altruism is not necessarily devoid of all personal rewards. An Unselfish lover experiences in return feelings of satisfaction, recognition, even gratitude. That is why there is usually some degree of agapic love in every good marriage and in every lasting relationship. Consider the story of a woman we'll call Anne:

"I married Alex thirteen years ago, and except for the first year of our marriage I haven't known what I consider a normal life. Alex was the son of parents who were terrified of change or insecurity. To please them he became an accountant—the kind of work his parents saw as safe and steady. But Alex couldn't stand doing a routine job, being shut in an office all day. He wanted to do something with his hands. He wanted to buy a ramshackle cottage in a rural area and remodel it himself. I was secretly terrified. Alex's job paid well, he'd been promised advancement—and I was pregnant and had my eye on a suburban home. But I knew Alex would suffocate there. So we lived in the woods and Alex modernized our cabin and hired out as a handyman/farm laborer to earn money. My baby was born and thrived, but a year later, again when I was pregnant, Alex said he wanted to move to California. We did. He worked as an accountant for a while, and I thought he might be ready to settle down, buy a house. But then the itch took him again, and I agreed to go with him to a logging town in the Yukon.

"To make a long story short, we have moved eight times and lived in three countries during our married life. By middle-class standards Alex is a failure. We don't own anything, we have no savings or pension plan, we have no roots, and we certainly don't have a predictable future. I can't say that is the way I wanted to live my life, or have it turn out. But Alex has been happy, and it has made me happy to give him the kind of life *he* wanted."

Those who follow the principles of Unselfish love, like Anne, try to live up to them as best they can. Failure to do so may cause guilt or self-disappointment. The philosopher Kierkegaard may have epitomized best the ultimate reward of an Unselfish love style: "The more one can sacrifice to love," he wrote, "the more interesting."

LOVE STYLES AND SEX DIFFERENCES

Is there any reason to believe that certain styles of love are more likely to be associated with men and other styles with women? Research indicates strongly that there is indeed a link between gender and love style.[6] Women are significantly more likely to be Logical, Possessive, or Best Friend lovers; men score significantly higher as Game Players and Romantics. There is little difference between the sexes so far as Unselfish love is concerned.

That women are more rational than men in their approach to love is a finding supported not only by a number of psychological studies but also by the common wisdom. Women have traditionally needed to consider whether their choices of love partners would prove to be considerate husbands and competent providers. In these liberated times, of course, when women are more self-sufficient economically, pregmatic concerns for security may not be important as they once were. Nevertheless, women are not so apt to fall romantically in love as men. Sociologist William Kephart once asked a thousand college students, all between the ages of eighteen and twenty-four: "If a man or woman had all the other qualities that you desired, would you marry this person if you were not in love with him or her?" Two out of every three men unequivocally answered, "No." But more than three out of every four women said they would.[7] "This contrast," Kephart observed, "again illustrates the male-female difference in romantic orientation. As one girl remarked: 'I'm undecided. But if a boy had all the other qualities I desired, and I was not in love with him—well, I think I could *talk* myself into falling in love!' "

Perhaps it is the fact that many people confuse sentiment with romanticism that has encouraged the illusion that women are romantics and men are hardheaded. Almost every sociological study during the past twenty years indicates that the reverse is true. Men tend to fall in love more quickly and to hold on longest when a relationship begins to crumble. It is usually the woman who takes the first steps toward ending an affair and the man who is most distressed when it does end. (After a disastrous love relationship, three times as many men as women commit suicide.) In their logical way, women seem more ready to accept the end of one love and to reorganize their lives. Men are not so easily resigned; they chew over the loss of love, wondering what they said or did wrong.

Possessive love is a style more common among women than among men, while Game Playing is more characteristically a male approach. Experts account for both of these findings on the basis of the traditional images of sex roles: women as jealous, demanding, and helpless; and men as Don Juans, selfishly toying with a woman's affections. In both cases, however, these sexual images are changing. As sex roles become more equalitarian women's love styles are shifting in the same direction, away from possessiveness and toward more playful love.

6

MIXED EMOTIONS

The good things of life are not to be had singly,
but come to us with a mixture.

—Charles Lamb, *Popular Fallacies*

She lives in one of the rustic canyons that weave through
the mountains north of the Los Angeles basin. Now in her
early fifties, she is a successful commercial artist by pro-
fession, an ardent bird watcher by avocation, and at times
an emotional puzzle to herself. Barbara (as we shall call
her) has been married twice, had one long and intense affair, and is about to marry again. None of those relationships was of the revolving-door stripe. Her first marriage
lasted seven years, her intimate liaison went on for three
years, and she lived contentedly with her second husband
for thirteen years before he died in a plane crash. Barbara
insists, and old friends bear witness, that she was deeply in
love with each of those men, and that she is equally in love
with the man she is going to marry.

"I know that in each case my feelings were sincere,"
Barbara says. "Yet I cannot understand how that can
be so. I grew up believing that you could really love
only one man in your lifetime. I knew that one could
be infatuated with a number of persons, and at least temporarily label that feeling as 'love.' But it always struck
me as ridiculous to claim that a woman could truly love
more than one man—and certainly not a succession of
men—equally well. Even now it upsets me to admit that
I have been able to do that. Am I essentially fickle? That
shallow? Or that callous? I can't believe I am any of
those things."

Indeed she isn't. Barbara is an example of the fact that
virtually every person has more than a single unalloyed

style of loving. Barbara's mixture of styles becomes evident when she describes—from the vantage points of both hindsight and emotional maturity—why she fell in love with each of the men in her life:

> "When I met Bill, my first husband, I was the only child of demanding and overprotective parents. I wanted desperately to escape, to be on my own. But I had little money, few skills, no self-confidence. I was sexually naïve. Marriage seemed to be the best and quickest way out of my parents' house, out of my dependency on them, out of my unworldliness."

Because a large part of her love style was Logical, Barbara found herself falling in love with the first man who could answer both her conscious and unconscious needs at the time. Bill was a successful businessman twice her age— still a comforting parental figure but one who, Barbara thought, would foster rather than threaten her independence. Bill, for his part, liked the idea of having a shy, dependent bride whom he could mold and teach. Unfortunately for Bill, he eventually answered Barbara's needs all too well. Logical lovers, you will recall, consider themselves in love only so long as they continue to perceive a relationship as a fair exchange of physical and emotional assets. But after several years of marriage Barbara began to feel she was putting more into her relationship with Bill than she was getting out of it. Her talents as a commercial artist had blossomed, and her free-lance services were now sought after by advertising agencies. She knew she could easily support herself if she had to. Her social skills had also matured, and her self-confidence had reached the point where she no longer needed her husband's backing.

At the same time Barbara was becoming aware of new and different needs. Marriage to Bill had not been, as she originally thought, an avenue to independence. Rather, she had merely substituted one dependency for another. And sex was still another area where the principle of "fair exchange" no longer held true. Bill, now in his late fifties, was not romantic or passionate enough for Barbara's burgeoning womanhood. She wanted more sexual excitement than Bill seemed able to provide. In the course of her work at that critical juncture Barbara met a handsome art director:

> "I think Arthur was the first man who really attracted me physically. At first I flirted with him for the fun of it—at least that's what I thought I was doing. When he politely but firmly refused to respond. I couldn't resist the challenge. I was determined to have Arthur, and of course I finally did."

The long affair with Arthur both reflected and stimulated a latent Game-Playing aspect of Barbara's love style. (As we shall see, the combination of Game Playing and Logical love is not uncommon.) But while the Game Player in her enjoyed the risks and challenges of illicit love, Barbara's Logical side was troubled. She could not see herself continuing to love Arthur, a man who offered absolutely no emotional guarantees beyond those of the moment. And she could not go on living with a husband for whom she now felt nothing beyond a mild gratitude. Barbara resolved the second concern by divorcing Bill. Resolving the first depended on Arthur's co-operation, but he proved to be too confirmed a Game Player:

> "He was not willing to make any sort of commitment to me," Barbara continues, "and after a few years our affair ended. Then there was quite a long period when I didn't go out with anyone. I had my work and my hobby, and I felt it was important to draw back into myself, to regroup my emotional forces. Understand, it was not that I was loveshy. Other people might call my experiences with Bill and Arthur failures, but I did not think of them that way. I had loved both men very much, and I wouldn't have missed what I had with each of them for anything."

Barbara's second marriage was to a man she met while on a bird-watching expedition to Central America:

> "Garrett and I fell in love under the most romantic circumstances you can imagine—a full moon over a tropical jungle, with all those strange sounds in the darkness. I didn't think it would last after we got home, but it did."

As Barbara describes the thirteen years of what she calls her most fulfilling relationship, one realizes that she and Garrett defined their ideas of love and loving in much the same way. While Garrett was primarily a Romantic, there was enough of the Game Player in his love style to prevent either him or Barbara from feeling emotionally fenced in or overpowered. Although they cared for each other deeply, both were sufficiently secure in themselves to tolerate apartness and to give each other as much freedom as each might desire. For the first time, one man was able to satisfy both the Logical and the Game-Playing elements —as well as a modest amount of the Romantic—which comprise Barbara's style of loving.

It has been five years since Garrett was killed in the crash landing of a commuter aircraft. Several months ago Barbara, who is now fifty-three, was introduced by mutual friends to a semi-retired, fifty-seven-year-old businessman:

> "I didn't think there would be anyone I could love after Garrett. But Tom is intelligent, kind, understanding. He reminds me a good deal of the way Bill was when I first knew him. Tom was divorced ten years ago and has been alone since then. I suppose we were drawn to each other out of our mutual need to find a congenial partner to share the years that are left to us. Old age is no time to be alone, and both Tom and I are intensely aware of that."

Barbara thus has come full circle in her approach to love. Realistically, she knows that her opportunities for Game Playing and Romanticism are going to be limited as she grows older. Tom meets her practical needs and she meets his in a special way. So Barbara is allowing the Logical aspect of her love style to take precedence, as it did in her first marriage.

Barbara's story illustrates a basic finding of love-style theory—the fact that almost no one has a single "pure" style of loving. Most men and women experience love in ways that reflect a combination of two and sometimes more styles. The styles may conflict with or reinforce one another; they may manifest themselves simultaneously or sequentially. They are at the root of what we call our "mixed emotions."

A few years ago, for example, a financial executive we know married a woman he carefully and logically chose because he decided that she had all the qualities necessary to be a good "corporation wife." This is not to say that he made a calculating choice divorced from feelings. He really did love the woman—but with a typically Logical approach he allowed himself to fall in love only with someone of her caliber. Though still happily married, the man recently began an affair with a young woman in his office. He has managed to maintain both relationships without alienating either his mistress, who knows he is married, or his wife, who suspects he is having an affair. The man's Love Scale profile—he scores high in both Logical and Game-Playing love and low in the other four categories—indicates not only why he is juggling two relationships but also how he has been able to do this so successfully. Both of his major love-style components characterize a cautious and somewhat manipulative emotional make-up. Not surprisingly, the executive is adept at compartmentalizing his feelings and his behavior. His low scores on Possessiveness, Unselfishness, and Romanticism indicate a lack of emotional intensity that serves the man well in these circumstances. If he felt more deeply about either his wife or his mistress, he would probably have trouble keeping the two relationships on their different stylistic levels. (If either of the women was strongly Possessive, she might unsettle this situation. Instead, the wife's concept of love is largely composed of Best Friend and Unselfish styles— the qualities for which her husband originally chose her. His mistress is high in the Romantic and Game-Playing aspects. Both therefore are able to adjust reasonably well to the arrangement the executive has constructed.)

Knowing that one's approach to love usually reflects a mixture of styles helps to explain how it is indeed possible to love more than one person at a time, like the executive; or, like Barbara, to love a succession of different people; or, like both of them, to be emotionally drawn to one person for one set of reasons and to another for quite a different set. Which style is emphasized or which becomes dominant at any given time seems to depend, as we shall see, on the partner's love style and the interplay between the two.

In order to explore the range of mixtures, we have paired the six so-called "pure" love styles into their fifteen

possible dual combinations. There are, of course, many
other potential combinations involving a complex mix of
three, four, or even more different styles. In most such instances, however, one or two of the styles still predom-
inate. If you have high scores on the Love Scale in more
than two categories, you will want to give attention to all
of the pairings that apply. But as you explore these mixtures it is important to remember that one playful experience does not a Game Player make, nor one possessive
act invalidate an Unselfish profile. It is the over-all and
continuing pattern that determines one's definition of love.

HIGH BEST FRIEND AND HIGH UNSELFISH

For you and for those whom you choose to love, this combination comes as close to an "ideal" style as one could
wish. If your scores indicate that you belong in this category you are a giver—one who invests the time and energy
to find out what the loved one really needs to make him
or her feel loved. You are usually patient and sensitive,
and expect to "be there" for your partner no matter when
or how he or she needs you. Your way of defining love is
to be undemanding, to try *not* to let your love get in the
other person's way. At the same time you are more likely
than most persons to understand and to accept the fact
that the one who loves you may not necessarily show that
love in the same ways you do. There is a risk in this approach to love: the other person may take advantage of
your selflessness. That's why you must choose a partner
carefully, so your style of loving behavior will not be misused or otherwise turned against you.

Deborah Franklin, Benjamin's wife, must surely have
defined love in this fashion. When they were first married
she took his illegitimate son into their home to raise as
her own. Shortly thereafter Franklin left her to run his
printing business and to raise their children while he shuttled between England and France, carrying out diplomatic
assignments. She even supervised the development of the
nation's postal system while Franklin, the official Post-
master General, was in Europe. Deborah Franklin's marriage was not easy on any count. While she was obliged
to remain faithful, her husband considered himself free to
have a number of sexual alliances. Yet as her letters show
she continued to be loyal, understanding, and affectionate.

Of course, as his correspondence to her reveals, Franklin loved Deborah too, but in his own more cavalier fashion. When Deborah fell ill Benjamin was, as usual, off somewhere tending to his own pursuits. She died alone. Franklin's letters to friends testify that he was deeply grieved. And no wonder; apart from anything else, not many men have had so giving and loving a partner.

Can this style of love still occur with any frequency in what has been labeled a "Me generation"? Indeed it can —and does. Quite often it is the unselfish, friendly love of one partner that enables the other to indulge his or her "me-ness." A thirty-six-year-old woman named Laura has a relationship with her husband that could be a modern version of Deborah Franklin's marriage to Ben. "My husband says he needs to get away, to have time alone," Laura says. "So when he goes off skiing or fishing I have to mind our hardware store myself. I'm not totally happy about it, but I accept it." Meanwhile, Pete confides that without these interludes of freedom he might not be able to stay married to Laura—or to any woman, for that matter. "Laura is a great person and we have a lot going in our relationship," Pete says. "I doubt that many women would put up with what she does. But I have to have the feeling of being free from time to time. If Laura couldn't let me have that I probably would have left her a long time ago."

Men and women with high Best Friend and Unselfish scores will have a happier time of it if they own a moderate amount of the Logical style as well. This would help them to make a more acute choice of partner. And if one is going to be a giving and unselfish lover, that is important, for it pays to pick a mate who will be worth it all.

HIGH BEST FRIEND AND HIGH LOGICAL

By taking on the added dimension of friendliness, the strictly practical outlook of the Logical love style is softened somewhat. If this is your mixture of styles, you are probably primarily interested in compatibility—in making as certain as you can that the person you choose to love shares most of your interests and values. As a result you tend to move rather cautiously toward deciding that you are in love. But so far as you are concerned there is no urgency about that. When you believe you have indeed found the right person you quietly cultivate the intimacy between you and your partner. If you have chosen a person who is similarly patient about the ripening of love, chances are a solid bond will grow between you.

You probably try to map out in some detail the ways in which your life with your partner will unfold. That helps to prevent surprises—and you don't like surprises, particularly from the one you love. While some people would be thrilled to find, tucked into a birthday card, two tickets to Singapore on a plane leaving in a week, a predominantly Logical lover might well be upset. We know one who was. It meant changing a host of his other plans. It did not fit into his schedule. It was a distinctly *il*logical interruption and, worst of all, he wasn't involved in planning the trip. You want to be in on all the planning in your love relationship to make sure the choices that are made are reasonable ones that will benefit both of you. The fact is that you don't leave much to chance in your love life; you act on logic rather than on feelings. Paradoxically, about the only time feelings are really likely to surface is when one of two contradictory conditions occurs: first, when all is going quite well and you can afford to relax your prudent concerns; and, second, when things are not going according to your expectations.

In our interviews with men and women who define love in this Best Friend/Logical fashion, we were struck by their highly organized approach to choosing a permanent partner. And the better the self-concept these people have of themselves, the higher they set their sights. For example, a colleague told us she had dated widely before she found the man to whom she was married for thirty years:

"I wanted to have a variety of experiences so I could be certain I *really* wanted what I *thought* I wanted in a man. I knew better than to marry early. I realized my tastes and values would change when I finished college and worked for a few years. I remember once I thought I found a man who was good husband material and brought him home to meet my parents. They disapproved. Not up to the standards of what I should have, they said. At the time I couldn't see why, so I continued to go out with him a while longer. One night my mother sarcastically said, 'Well, all right, Martha, settle for him; perhaps he's the best you can do.' That was like a slap in my face, but suddenly I saw she was right. I *could* do better. I broke off with the man right away. I knew I'd made the right decision when, a few months later, I met the man I did marry."

HIGH BEST FRIEND AND HIGH ROMANTIC

This seems an unlikely mixture—on the one hand the gradual development of liking into loving that characterizes the Best Friend, and on the other the swift emotional and physical involvement with an idealized partner that characterizes the Romantic. Nevertheless, the combination does occur with surprising frequency. But if you are like most men and women who have this compound of styles, you are aware of its inherent contradictions. You often must struggle to prevent Romantic feelings from leading you too precipitately into love relationships which your calmer judgment warns may later prove inappropriate. You may have to guard yourself against moving too quickly, against becoming too committed until your Best Friend aspect has a chance to get to know the other person better. "I have fallen in love many times," says one woman with this combination, "but I always knew there were very few men I could actually like well enough to stay with. That saved me from making some serious mistakes."

In essence, you have to like the person you love and love the person you like—a tall order. However, when the initial Romantic attraction does deepen into friendship, this can be one of the most rewarding combinations of styles. You believe that sentiment or passion alone is not enough for love to survive the complexities of a relationship. But neither will you settle for merely a good friendship: The Romantic feelings must maintain their overtones or you will always sense something lacking. Virginia Satir, a well-known family therapist, describes that as the feeling "that I could matter enough to another person, and that person could matter enough to me, so that when things are tough we could somehow fall back on this romantic connection. . . ." (Conversely, if romantic passion fades —as it usually must over time—friendship continues to provide the glue in the relationship.)

For the most part, the Best Friend aspect of this combination tends to dominate. But when Romantic needs surface they must be released or met. The wife of a man with this definition of love reports that when she makes a business trip out of town she often finds that her husband has ordered flowers sent to brighten her hotel room. The card reads simply, "I love you." Since she, too, has a high Romantic element in her love style, she usually picks up the telephone to tell him, "I love you too."

HIGH BEST FRIEND AND HIGH GAME PLAYING

This is another seemingly paradoxical combination. It is as if one seeks a steadfast companion who will at the same time provide a challenge at the game of love. A veteran tennis pro whose Love Scale score produced this result likened his feelings about emotional relationships to his feelings about a tennis partner:

> "It's no fun to play with someone who can always beat me. But it's worse to play with someone who isn't in my league at all. I want a partner who will keep me on my toes, give me an even match. Otherwise there is no challenge. I have one tennis partner I've played with for ten years. In the hundreds of matches we've played, I don't think either of us has ever been more than a couple of games ahead. So I'm not surprised that I feel the same about love as I do about tennis. If the rewards come too easily I get bored and begin to look for a more challenging partner. That's one thing about my wife— she's never boring."

This attitude is consistent with research on learning theory. If rewards are predictable and easily obtained, they lose some of their effectiveness. We seem to respond better to inconsistency and to challenge. If your score adds up to this love-style mixture, chances are you seek a partner with whom you can be secure in the knowledge that both of you are together out of free choice—because you *want* to be rather than because you *need* to be. If you are like most people in this category you will have had an emotionally secure childhood. Not necessarily an ideally happy one—there may have been bad with the good, but you have been able to accept that. As a result you are secure now in your approach to other loving relationships. One woman put it this way: "Take any quality I have—looks, brains, personality, enthusiasm in bed, skill in the kitchen. I know there's bound to be some woman somewhere who is prettier or smarter or sexier than I am. But if you're talking about the whole package, my husband would search a long time to find a woman who is all-around better for him than I am. And I feel the same way about him. We're a good match."

Men and women with this combination find that they get along best with a partner who has the same or a similar pattern. Each of them must have enough self-confidence to stand up to the challenge the other will present and to provide the challenge the other will want. That is not to say they do not understand or respect the need for commitment in love. But they do not permit commitment to lull them into emotional complacency. A woman who is herself a whirlwind of activity—a teacher, part-time travel agent, active community worker, mother of three teen-agers—said she felt lucky to have found the man she married:

"Oh, he's difficult at times, but he is never, never dull. He works hard, he plays hard, he drinks hard. And all of that can be hell to live with sometimes. But he has an exciting mind. And he's willing to try new things. He has run for public office. He learned to pilot a plane. He's a fierce competitor in everything he does. I look at some of my women friends and I wonder why they aren't dying of boredom. Their husbands may be nicer than mine—but they never *do* anything!"

In a good match your partner will offer as much challenge as you need. If he or she fails to do that, you might be tempted to seek new or different stimuli. But you are basically interested in testing the limit of the possibilities for fulfillment with the partner you have—so long as he or she continues to keep the game interesting.

HIGH BEST FRIEND AND HIGH POSSESSIVE

A relatively uncommon mixture of styles, this takes the form of a dependent friendship. You demand exclusivity from a partner and tend to be jealous of his or her friends, family, or other interests. You don't like being separated from your partner physically. At a dinner party it would not be out of character for you to object to being seated at a distance from him or her; and though you might be involved in a conversation in one corner of the room, you would keep part of your attention focused on what your partner was doing in another corner. This may seem to be the profile of an unalloyed Possessive, but your motivations are quite different. Neither fear, lack of self-esteem, jealousy, nor a wish to control is the major reason for your behavior. The simple fact is that you enjoy being with your partner better than being with anyone else, and you see no reason to be separated. If you are married, you may never have spent a night away from your spouse. If circumstances forced you to be apart, you probably felt lonely and miserable. It is hard for you to understand how couples who love each other can ever take separate vacations. Since a Best Friend style implies concern for the other person's emotional needs, combining it with Possessiveness presents a problem if the partner's needs include a degree of independence and freedom. How well you can accept that depends greatly on your own self-confidence. The surer you are about yourself the more able you will be to minimize your desire for total togetherness.

HIGH ROMANTIC AND HIGH POSSESSIVE

A great deal has been written about this mixture of styles, most of it unflattering. It is the catalyst of countless romantic novels and "If I can't have you nobody can!" melodramas. Carmen (most likely a Game-Playing lover if indeed she could love at all) meets her doom at the hands of the Romantic-Possessive Don José; Othello in his jealous love kills Desdemona; Scarlett O'Hara's proprietary ways finally alienate Rhett Butler.

Psychologists are familiar with the problems of men and women who find exactly the partner they've been waiting for but then become so dependent and possessive that they risk destroying—or actually do destroy—the relationship. The conventional wisdom says that these qualities are hallmarks of emotional insecurity, that this style of love is not love at all but the acting out of a neurosis. To be sure, there are many neurotic attachments that masquerade in the guise of love. But we believe that the combination of romanticism and possessiveness validly reflects what many people normally feel when they say they are in love.

Consider the following statement drawn from an interview with a young woman who has this combination of scores:

"I am jealous of my fiancé beyond belief. When we are together somewhere and an attractive woman appears, I feel very anxious and will do anything to distract him. I attach myself to him, reminding him that I am there. Of course, I know he really loves me—but I take no chances. When he's away from me there's nothing more important on my mind than wondering what he is doing. I expect at least two calls a day from him. If he's late calling, I'll call him. If he doesn't tell me he loves me and misses me, I feel really depressed. We didn't see each other for three days, and despite the gasoline shortage I couldn't stand it. I drove fifty miles each way to take him a cake I baked. My father nearly had a fit. But that's what love is all about, isn't it?"

Despite the misery attributed to such lovers by psychologists and writers, the men and women we talked with were definite in their belief that they could not truly *be* in love unless they experienced the intensity of feeling created by this mixture of styles. These people were not particularly insecure, nor did they have miserable love lives. Most had learned to survive the painful moments and enjoyed the Romantic-Possessive dependency they felt for the ones they loved. Unlike a purely Possessive lover, men and women with this combination rarely make trouble where none exists. But they can react in that way if they are threatened with separation. In one case, a naval officer was granted a discharge when his wife had a "nervous breakdown" during his first stint of sea duty. The navy psychiatrist's recommendation for the man's release produced a total remission of the woman's symptoms.

HIGH ROMANTIC AND HIGH GAME PLAYING

Karen is thirty-eight but she looks ten years younger. She has had a brief marriage and, since it ended, a series of love affairs—"warm, even intense, but never anything I couldn't get out of with a whole skin," she says. About two years ago she began living with Paul, who is several years younger than she. Now Paul wants to marry her, but Karen is reluctant to make that commitment. "I have exactly what I want right now," she says. "If we were to marry it might change everything. You begin to take each other too casually. The way it is now, Paul can never be quite sure of me, nor I of him. I have always felt that is what keeps the sparks alive." Karen pauses, then reluctantly concedes, "On the other hand I love Paul more than any man I've known, and I don't want to lose him."

Karen's dilemma is typical of this love-style mixture. Until she met Paul her Game-Playing side was in charge. Karen never really "fell in love" so much as she enjoyed the companionship of diverting partners. Now the Romantic aspect of her style has drawn her into a more intense relationship. One part of her yearns for permanence and commitment, another part fears the vulnerability which that implies. How Karen resolves her conflict will depend to a great extent on how she feels about herself. If she has sufficient self-esteem to believe that she is truly worth being loved she will probably be able to risk making the commitment.

If your Love Scale score indicated this as your combination of styles, you are likely to be seen by your partner(s) as a changeable lover—sometimes capable of intense intimacy, sometimes insistent on a more detached relationship. You may be accused of coldness but the accusation is usually unfounded. You are, rather, self-contained—a person who can enjoy a warm and close love relationship so long as you feel you will not be badly hurt if it ends, or even if it does you know you will survive to love again. Some persons with this pattern find an outlet for both the Romantic and Game-Playing elements by remaining committed to one love partner while pursuing a purely erotic relationship with another. Since they are usually willing to grant a partner the same freedom, they don't see why anyone should object.

HIGH ROMANTIC AND HIGH UNSELFISH

This combination represents not only a popularly accepted defintion of love but one that many humanistic thinkers defend as the authentic definition. Aristotle was among those who believe that in "real" love one lives only for the loved one's sake. Thus when Leander drowns while swimming the Hellespont to be with Hero, Hero throws herself in the sea to join her lover in death. Romeo, believing Juliet to be dead, takes poison; Juliet, seeing Romeo dead, stabs herself. Most who love in this style are fortunately not called upon to make the ultimate sacrifice. But they do give their all by subordinating their feelings to the needs of the lover, by fulfilling his or her wishes at the expense of their own. "When I met Jim I wanted nothing more than to please him," a young woman says. "I was overwhelmingly attracted to him from the start, but I think even if I hadn't felt that way I could not have refused anything he asked me. I can't imagine going on without him. Still, if it came to a choice between Jim's happiness and mine I would be more concerned about his. If that meant letting him go, I honestly think I could do it."

The Romantic/Unselfish mixture is partially responsible for many of the "martyr" relationships therapists often see. A woman wastes her youth waiting for her hoodlum lover to reform; a man puts up for years with an alcoholic wife, deluding himself that someday she will stop drinking. Indeed, such men and women seem able to fall in love *only* with someone deeply troubled, someone who needs to be "rescued." They are driven by the belief that eventually their kind of love will help the partner to change. Ironically, on those rare occasions when that *does* happen the Romantic/Unselfish partner is likely to find that he or she no longer "loves" the other. With no more sacrifices to make, what is the point in loving?

HIGH ROMANTIC AND HIGH LOGICAL

"The people I fall in love with always turn out to be wrong for me," says Sheilah, a recently divorced attorney. After the breakup of her second marriage she vowed not to become romantically involved again. "But how can I exist without being in love?" she asks. Sheilah's dilemma is characteristic of people with this love-style mixture. They often feel confused as they struggle to make sense out of their emotional attraction to someone they know is logically 'wrong' for them. Unlike some other combinations of love styles, the Romantic and the Logical are more likely to strive against each other than to blend. First one element will dominate and then the other. When reason is consciously called into play it has little trouble taking over. John Lee found, for example, that when a person analyzes a love relationship in terms of its advantages and disadvantages romantic feelings have little influence on the outcome. But when romantic feelings are given their head, logic is casually cast aside.

Sheilah's story is a case in point. She met Carl, who became her second husband, when she joined a health and exercise club. Carl was a physical fitness instructor there. "He had a wonderful body," Sheilah said. "I think I fell in love with all those muscles. One night I had a small party so my friends could meet Carl. The next day my oldest friend called and asked if I was out of my mind. 'What do you mean?' I said. 'Falling for a lug like Carl,' she replied. 'He's not what you need, he's not your kind of man.' One part of me knew she was right," Sheilah continued, "but another part of me didn't care."

Sheilah and Carl were married for two years before she left him. "It took that long for me to be able to admit to myself that he isn't the kind of man I need," she said. "He likes to go back-packing. He wanted me to go jogging with him every day and he couldn't understand it when I said that I'd rather use the little leisure time I have to catch up on my reading. We used to fight a lot about that." Sheilah smiled a bit sadly. "Look, Carl's a great guy. He just didn't fit into my life, that's all. I need a man who is sophisticated, who can talk to my friends, who can move with me comfortably in my professional world. I know that now—and I guess I knew it when I married Carl. But, damnit, I *did* love him!"

In another case a college professor of literature—married for fifteen years and the father of two children—fell passionately in love with a student in one of his freshman classes. The young woman, flattered and excited by the power she had over a mature and intelligent man, responded eagerly. The professor asked a counselor to help him work out his tormented feelings.

"There is every reason in the world for me to end this relationship," he said. "I'm old enough to be the girl's father. I love my wife and my children. I know it's crazy to risk my job and reputation this way. I have responsibilities, principles, even religious convictions.

But I can't stop seeing her. I even dream about her. And I also know there's no future in it, I know she'll tire of me pretty soon, or find someone her own age. *What am I going to do?"*

So long as the girl was available the professor's struggle to give her up did not succeed. Finally her parents, aware of the situation, sent her abroad for a year. For the first few months the lovers kept in touch through letters and phone calls. But gradually the young woman responded less frequently and less intensely. In a final letter she explained that she had met a young man and fallen in love with him. "It was wonderful while it lasted, but please don't write or call me any more," she wrote. Like a drug addict sentenced to a cold-turkey cure, the professor suffered through agonizing days of romantic yearning. Had he had more of the Romantic in him, he might have followed the young woman to Europe. As it was, once the emotional pain lessened and then disappeared altogether, he felt considerably relieved.

It seems to be extraordinarily difficult, if not impossible, to blend the Romantic and Logical styles into a cohesive and functional whole. Unless, that is, you happen to be lucky enough to fall head over heels in love with someone who just happens to turn out to be a perfectly logical partner for you. This is what everyone with this style hopes will be the case. For most people with this style, however, love is likely to be a source of sustained conflict and confusion about what they feel ought to be and what is. No matter which style prevails at any given time, they are likely to experience some sense of regret that the other one has not overruled it—or a sense of relief that it has.

HIGH GAME PLAYING AND HIGH POSSESSIVE

Like the previous combination of styles, this does not make for a felicitous blend. There is bound to be a great deal of ambivalence: on the one hand the desire for an easygoing love relationship based on challenge and the risk of loss, and on the other a fear of loss that often leads to self-defeating anxiety. A man or woman with this style may even be trapped between a Game Player's wish to end a relationship and a Possessive's need to hang onto it. "I can't seem to let old lovers go," a seemingly shy but provocatively dressed woman observed. "I have no trouble meeting new men, but I'm always afraid that I *will* have. When it's time to break off I keep wondering if I won't regret letting the man go. Maybe I won't find anyone I'll like as well." Some therapists believe this need to cling to a lover stems from self-doubt and fears of loneliness. This may be, but we tend to think it more likely reflects the underlying assumption of all Possessives that a relationship without a touch of obsession cannot be love in the first place.

HIGH GAME PLAYING AND HIGH LOGICAL

Some Logical lovers can enjoy a challenge and some Game Players are pragmatic in the choice of partners. The combination of these styles produces an individual who tends to be less deliberate and controlled than the chiefly Logical lover, but more willing to make concessions to a partner than the Game-Playing type. If you have this combination you probably avoid intense emotions because you believe they will cloud your judgment. You suspect there are a number of people you could love and that it is only a matter of time until the right partner appears. Should the one you choose not measure up to your expectations, you may circumspectly begin to search for someone you think does. This is not to say that you will not put effort into making your present relationship work. You will—but only up to a point. Logic will determine for you where that point is. The greater the practical stakes in the partnership, the greater the effort you will make to maintain it.

If you were to be entirely honest about it, you would probably agree that love is not the most important thing in the world to you. You are more likely to fit it in among your other interests. In fact your approach to a loving relationship may be so coolly self-controlled that even close friends may wonder whether you actually *can* love anyone, or if you *do* love your partner. But you know.

HIGH GAME PLAYING AND HIGH UNSELFISH

Only a small percentage of men and women have this lovestyle profile. If you are one of them, you probably have a strong tendency to idealize the concept of love—to have been taught that it is supposed to be an all-giving relationship. Yet you hesitate to act on this basis lest you be swallowed up by a partner. "I may be too selfish to be married," said one man who did not yet know that he had scored high on the Unselfish scale. "I know that when you're in love you are supposed to put the other person's needs ahead of your own. But I can't do that consistently. I feel as if I would be 'nobody' if I was always the one to yield." Yet, like this man, you may feel guilty when you hold yourself back from a giving relationship. "It's something like playing chess with my young son," a man commented. "I can beat him easily, so to compensate I let him win a lot of the time. But then I find myself resenting that. I'm the same way with a woman. For a while I want to give her everything she desires. Then, suddenly, I'll get angry for being such a sucker. I guess it isn't really loving at all to feel that way, is it?"

It is also possible to appear to be unselfish yet to be giving only what you do not care about. A successful executive boasted of the sacrifices he made for his wife and children. He worked hard to give them every material advantage—cars, servants, travel, the best schools and summer camps. To provide those luxuries, however, the man claimed he had to devote virtually all his time to business. He worked most nights and many weekends and rarely could join his family on the trips he arranged for them. In effect he was giving them everything but himself —using "unselfishness" as a distancing technique to avoid the intimate commitment the Game-Playing side of him feared.

HIGH LOGICAL AND HIGH POSSESSIVE

If this is your combination of styles you are probably acutely aware of the conflicts inherent in it. Though your love affairs may begin in a rational way, they tend to create a sense of dependency which makes you uncomfortable. You see it as a flaw in your personality. If the Logical side of your emotional nature feels trapped by the Possessive, it may attempt to break the impasse by becoming superlogical—by ferreting out a real or fancied defect in the other person. With that as a focal point, you are often able to decide that the relationship is not so much worth clinging to as you originally thought. The prospect of losing the partner is not quite so distressing. It is as if the Logical component of this love style has reminded the Possessive that it is not completely in control.

HIGH LOGICAL AND HIGH UNSELFISH

This is a particularly interesting mixture since it attempts a delicate balancing act. If this is your style you define love as being a giver to a carefully chosen partner. The secret of success lies in selecting a person whose wants and needs will not seem unreasonable to you and will, in so far as possible, match your capacity to meet them. You are realistic enough to know there will be times when a partner's needs will exceed your ability or willingness to give. But you expect these periods to be temporary. You are not about to accept a relationship involving constant or inordinate self-sacrifice as a purely Unselfish lover would.

Not long ago we spoke at a university seminar for women who were seeking to redefine their roles as housewives and mothers. All of the participants were wrestling with the questions of whether, when, and how their personal fulfillment should take precedence over their husbands' and children's needs. The women who proved to have this Logical-Unselfish style of love were particularly troubled about the "selfish" aspect of self-fulfillment. They appreciated their affluent life styles, but they were also aware of having given up opportunities for self-growth in order to further their husbands' careers. The message from the experts conducting the seminar was: "Consider your own needs first for a change. You have been unselfish long enough. Remember that if you aren't happy no one around you will be either." But to the women with this love style the troubling question was: "Can I be happy if I am not being giving?" Most of them realized they had chosen to put the family's needs ahead of their own because it made them more psychologically comfortable. If they were "victims" of unselfishness it was largely their own fault. Unlike some of the others in the seminar, these women will probably not make basic changes in their ways of living and loving. But they do need to redefine their concept of unselfish behavior so as not to feel victimized by it.

HIGH UNSELFISH AND HIGH POSSESSIVE

This most mutually contradictory of love-style combinations is also the rarest. So few men and women who have been tested show this profile that research data on it are virtually non-existent. It is our impression, however, that anyone who attempts to love in this way would have an enormous internal conflict. To require everything from a partner and at the same time be willing to give everything in return is possible, we feel, only if both partners share this same combination of styles. Even so it is likely to be a fragile relationship, highly vulnerable to hurt and disappointment.

The few instances of this mixture that we encountered reminded us of the image of the "bird in the gilded cage." For example, one man said he found it easier to be generous to his lover when she was cut off from her family and friends. In essence, that reinforced his sense of possession while at the same time giving him the opportunity to be the only person available to meet the woman's needs. Another case involved a woman who volunteered to be a pen pal to prisoners in a state penitentiary. She began to correspond regularly with one man, eventually visited him, and fell in love with him. Though he has six years still to serve, the woman has made up her mind to marry him when he is released. Meanwhile she is saving her money so she can support them until he finds work. Clearly, this is a long-term project in unselfishness. Yet at the same time the prison bars guarantee that the man will not be able to get away from her control. The moral is self-evident: the need to possess another can also involve the need to nurture him or her; conversely, benevolent behavior may cloak the need to possess.

It is important to keep in mind that, just as no single love style is "good" or "bad," "right" or "wrong," neither is any of these combinations of styles. Partners with styles that mesh will find their relationship more satisfying than those whose styles conflict. But "different" is not the same thing as "wrong." Each style and mixture of styles is equally valid. There is no one correct way to love.

7

THE SEXUAL MEANINGS
OF LOVE STYLES

The . . . process of sex is the pattern of all the
process of our life.

—Havelock Ellis, *The New Spirit*

Why are some men and women sexually impetuous while
others are sexually patient? Why is one person aroused
sexually by a lover's rejection, or by the lash of jealousy,
while another is sexually depressed by such reactions? Why
do certain partners remain faithful to one another while
others succumb to temptation or actively instigate infidelities? Why do some lovers seek variety in their sex
lives—different environments, different techniques, different partners—while others prefer the security of a sexual
pattern to which they are accustomed?

Such wide variation in individual sexual attitudes and
actions can flow from many sources: personality traits,
early experiences with the way our emotional needs were
met or not met, and the images and illusions we hold about
our sexual identity. Some experts speak of "sexual scripts"
that govern people's intimate lives—in effect, psychological
programming which prompts our sexual expectations and
behavior. Nor does the list end there. Each person learns
in a different way to recognize sexual excitement and to
link it with specific situations and partners. Some of us
learn to translate feelings of love into sexual arousal;
others learn to translate arousal into feelings of love.
Moreover, there are enormous individual differences in the
way we pick and respond to sexual signals. Some men and
women have a limited repertoire; for them, perhaps, only
specific kinds of touching trigger the process. For others,
a variety of signals—visual cues, fantasies, provocative
books and films, certain fabrics and odors—are sexual
stimulants.

In addition to all of these factors, we now know that different styles of loving also put their imprint on one's sexual stance. When partners fail to realize or recognize that each style carries its own set of sexual meanings, love and sex can sometimes make strange bedfellows. For example, a distressed young husband recently brought this problem to a sex therapist:

"My wife and I lived together for a year before we married, and during all that time sex was exciting and satisfying for both of us. But right after the wedding this woman, who had been so passionate in bed before, suddenly became almost completely uninterested in sex. Now she finds endless excuses to avoid making love. When she finally agrees, she behaves in such a way that the whole experience is perfunctory and mechanical. My wife says she still loves me, but she refuses to discuss why her sexual feelings have changed. When I say I feel cheated she gets angry."

In another instance a woman lodges another traditional complaint:

"Since our marriage my husband has been far less affectionate than he was during our courtship. Sex isn't the problem; he is always ready for that. But being loving is another matter. He denies that there have been any changes in his feelings, or his actions. It is possible he is unaware of the difference between the way he was then and the way he is now?"

Neither of these situations is particularly unusual. The most common explanation offered for them is the cynical "Well, she (or he) got what she wanted. Why bother to keep up the act after you're married?" There may be a touch of self-defeating truth in that interpretation. But most men and women are not good enough actors to carry out an emotional or sexual charade over a long period of time. It seems far more reasonable to seek explanations in other areas, especially the sexual attributes of the various styles of love. For example, to some lovers, especially those whose styles emphasize the Game-Playing components, the novelty of discovering a partner physically, and the challenge of conquering him or her sexually, are often major factors in sexual interest and excitement. For others, a sense of risk or the knowledge that the sex they are having is by conventional standards illicit can be a similar turn-on.

Thus the woman who suddenly became uninterested in love-making after marriage may well have unconsciously allowed other elements in her love style to emerge once her relationship was legitimized. With these new elements comes a different attitude toward sex. In her new role as wife this woman may see herself in quite a different sexual light—perhaps as a partner with equal say about the couple's sexual frequency rather than as an always accommodating sex object. If there is a strong Best Friend element to her love style, she may feel that the erotic aspect of her nature should be subordinated now to her new role of companion and friend. Motherhood—even the thought of potential motherhood—causes some women to repress their sexual selves under the illusion that sex does not fit the maternal image.

If the husband who feels "cheated" is a Possessive lover he may interpret his wife's sexual resistance as a sign of some loss of emotional control over her. On the other hand, if there was a large amount of the Romantic in his love make-up, the man could feel his wife's new attitude was fitting. For many Romantics tend to act out their style only to certain appropriate cues—in courtship and early marriage, say, with periodic revivals on vacations, birthdays, and wedding anniversaries. But most likely this husband might cling to sentimental but exaggerated memories of what the couple's love-making was like before they were married. Compared to memories, present realities often cannot help but be disappointing.

In this second instance, the wife who feels emotionally neglected may similarly be indulging in extravagant Romantic recollections of her husband's earlier behavior. But it is also possible that marriage made the man feel freer to indulge the previously restrained Logical side of his love style. As a result, he can now act on the practical assumption that, since he has demonstrated his love by marrying the woman, he no longer has to convey his feelings by open displays of affection. He may believe that being a good provider or a good parent is more important. Frequently the sheer fact of having regular sexual access to one's partner—without the need to plan for it, hope for it, or go through the minuet of courtship for it—is sufficient in itself to dull the edge of romance. Thus this husband may be a Game Player who, with no more need to play games, loses some of his interest, or he may be unconsciously permitting Best Friend feelings to dominate his love style now that the marriage seems on solid ground.

As we noted earlier, Freud believed that love developed only when the sex drive was blocked from achieving its fleshly goal. He defined love, you will recall, as "aim-inhibited sex"—an idealized emotion that arises out of sexual frustration and loses its intensity when the frustration is overcome. Accordingly, there should be a positive correlation between sexual restrictiveness and Romantic love. Though this theory has been largely rejected or ignored in recent years, some evidence for it exists in studies of sexual patterns in a variety of cultures. For instance, Tahitian customs or morality at one time imposed no sexual restrictions of any kind. From puberty on, men and women alike could sleep guiltlessly with anyone they pleased. Free of any overtones of love, intercourse was valued exclusively for the pleasure it offered. But with no obstacles to sexual consummation, Tahitians were among the least romantic people on the earth. As an anthropologist put it: "Tahitians have no word to describe romantic love . . . and the exclusive union of two souls rather than two bodies would strike a Tahitian as utterly ridiculous."[1] Ancient Rome was another culture in which the absence of prohibitions against sex seemed to subvert romanticism. When Rome's sexual rules and customs grew increasingly permissive, points out author Morton Hunt, the sentiment of love became almost incidental to a sexual relationship. Ultimately there was almost no linkage at all between them. Sexual relationships, Hunt writes, were "lusty, exuberant, and unclouded by a sense of sin, but . . . strangely blended with obscenity, and hatred; [love] burned brightest between lovers who quarreled, tormented each other, and were flagrantly unfaithful."[2] Conversely, medieval courtly love—based, as we have seen, on an extreme ideal of sexual inhibition and frustration—became the source and forerunner of romanticism. A knight would serve his lady for many years knowing that the only regard of love he might eventually receive would be a single kiss. If he were supremely devoted and truly favored, he might ultimately win the right to caress her nude body—with the understanding that the act of sex itself was forbidden. Never before or since has Freud's definition of love been so widely and accurately realized.

An interesting sidelight on the correlation between sexual restrictiveness and romantic love is provided by a study of love lyrics in American song hits. Popular songs written in the conservative era between the mid-1950s and mid-1960s used adjectives such as "angel," "heavenly," or "pretty" to describe a loved one twice as often as songs written in the late 1970s. In this sexually liberated era, lyrics are more likely to extol the earthy pleasures of physical love.[3] With sex so available, why bother to romanticize?

SEXUAL BEHAVIOR PROFILES

With the caveat that "pure" love styles rarely exist and that individual responses may vary considerably from the following generalized descriptions, let's look at the typical sexual behavior profile that can be drawn for each of the six basic love styles.

Physical attraction and the urgency of sexual intimacy are usually of secondary importance to the *Best Friend lover*. Since his or her feelings of love develop slowly and almost imperceptibly, erotic interest in a partner occurs relatively late in a relationship. Love-making is seen as the culmination of a ripening friendship, a physical sign of emotional commitment. When it does take place, however, it is accepted comfortably and joyously. Such a gradual approach to sex does not imply any lack of interest or passion in a Best Friend lover. Rather, it reflects his or her basic feeling that love grows through a series of increasingly revealing self-disclosures and that, since sex is one of the most intimate of such revelations, it is neither useful nor tasteful to rush into it.

Because a Best Friend lover does not invest sex with overwhelming importance, he or she can tolerate ups and downs in the sexual side of a love relationship more easily than most other people. Elizabeth, who is thirty-two years old and has been married for seven years, typifies this quality:

"Neither my husband nor I was experienced sexually when we decided to marry. The first year of physical adjustment to each other was difficult. We did resolve the major problems, but even so there are still many times in our marriage when sex is not satisfactory for one or the other of us. I know some couples in a situation like this might decide to call it quits. But we have something else going for us, something we both consider more important than sex. That is the feeling of emotional closeness between us. Even when the sexual side of our marriage is disappointing there are enough other things, like trust and affection, to hold us together. That more than makes up for whatever we might be missing in bed."

Simone de Beauvoir's love relationship of more than fifty years with Jean-Paul Sartre illustrates this Best Friend approach to sex. She tells how they each have had other sex partners over the years yet have kept their pact never to leave each other—a pact they made when Sartre was twenty-three and De Beauvoir was twenty-one. She says: "I've sometimes wondered if he got along with such and such a woman better than with me. But once you know there is something irreplaceable between you and another person, many things become unimportant."[4] For the Best Friend lover, then, sex takes its place as only one of many aspects of the relationship.

The Game-Playing lover enjoys a playful and flirtatious sexual world and is likely to treat sex in a deceptively casual way. He or she considers it just another facet of the game of love, another counter to be moved about on the playing board for tactical advantage. "Winning" the game may involve seducing the other person into a physical relationship. But the achievement (or the act) of sexual intimacy itself does not usually matter as much as the fact of having successfully maneuvered the affair to that end. People who refer to a sexual conquest as a "score" unwittingly reflect this Game-Playing attitude.

Unlike the Romantic lover, the Game Player does not consider physical attractiveness essential for a sexual relationship. "[He] notices differences between bodies," says John Alan Lee, "but thinks it is stupid to specialize. . . .

When he is not near the girl he loves, he loves the girl he's near."[5] Surprisingly, most Game Players are not likely to be sophisticated in sexual matters or concerned about improving their sexual techniques. Each one tends to have his or her basic sexual approach. If it succeeds, fine. If not, the playful lover reasons, it is easier to find a new partner than to try to work out sexual problems with an old one. If a woman doesn't like his sexual pattern, the Game-Playing man simply moves on to someone else; if a man cannot satisfy her sexually, the Game-Playing woman looks for a partner who will. (Or he or she may enjoy sexual experimentation *within* a firm relationship.)

On the other hand, if sex becomes too significant or too satisfying a part of a relationship, a Game Player may come to think of it as a threat to his or her style of loving: "I enjoyed going to bed with Lois until I realized how important sex with her was becoming to me," one man said. "I didn't want to be trapped by that kind of a dependency." It is as if, wrote psychoanalyst Theodor Reik, "the ego were afraid of a . . . threatening loss."

For the Game-Playing lover, then, the rewards of sexual closeness and fulfillment tend to become overshadowed by the looming menace of commitment. As a result, sex is likely to be a self-centered pastime. The lover is intent on making sure that physical intimacy does not narrow the emotional distance he or she endeavors to maintain —even from the partner who is cared about the most. One woman engaged to a Game Player was so baffled by what was to her such a paradoxical attitude that shortly before their wedding she took her puzzlement and hurt to a marriage counselor. At twenty-eight, Jill was no stranger to her generation's sexual mores. She had experimented sexually with a number of partners and had lived with one lover for almost a year before that relationship ended. Now, however, she was deeply in love with the man she planned to marry.

Jill: We've been engaged for six months and I haven't slept with anyone else during that time.
Marcia Laswell: Was that part of an agreement between you? Did you discuss any rules for sexual behavior, or set any limits for each other?

Jill: No, I didn't think that was necessary. I knew how I felt about Liam, and when I made that kind of commitment my sexual loyalty automatically became part of it. But evidently he doesn't feel that way at all. Every time he comes back from a business trip he seems to get some peculiar kick out of telling me how he met a girl and went to bed with her.

M.L.: And how do you react to that?

Jill: I know . . . I suppose I should ignore it, not give him the satisfaction of rising to the bait. But I can't. I get angry, and I say so. I tell him that if I am faithful he ought to be too. But Liam says there is no such thing as being "unfaithful" so long as we aren't married. Would he feel that way if he really loved me?

M.L.: The fact that Liam sleeps with other women may have nothing to do with how much he loves you. But you and he seem to be operating with two incompatible sets of rules. You rather obviously feel you are as good as married and should accept the obligation to fidelity that goes with that. Liam evidently believes that until a wedding ceremony takes place he still has the right to live by the code of a single person. Have you talked over your different views from this standpoint?

Jill: I guess I've mostly been accusing him. I've been too upset to discuss it rationally. Mostly what Liam says is that he feels trapped by my demands.

M.L.: It's possible that by sleeping with other women he is in effect saying, both to you and to himself, "See, I'm still free, I'm not really locked in yet, I still have choices." There are certain people who need to feel that way.

Jill: So what should I do?

M.L.: Well, if Liam isn't ready to commit himself fully to you until he's actually standing at the altar and saying "I do," it does raise the question of just how much of a commitment he is ready to make. You've been engaged for six months and he hasn't yet decided to be sexually loyal. You may want to think about postponing the wedding until he shows he's more ready for it. But Liam may be the kind of man who will keep on fighting that "trapped" feeling even after marriage. It's not that he doesn't love you. But some people, when they feel too bound to a partner, need to re-establish their sense of separateness. If Liam is one of these, you may be in for a lifetime of having him pull away every time he feels that he has gotten too close.

In the Logical love style, sex is usually neither more nor less important than any of the other major factors that affect relationships. The typical Logical lover is always aware of his or her basic values and deals with sex primarily by measuring its plusses or minuses against the context of those values. "To me," said a man who defines love in this pragmatic way, "sex is just one of many threads in the overall pattern of a partnership." If a Logical lover's sex life is less than satisfying, but most other aspects of a relationship are rewarding, he or she will probably decide to give sexual activity a lower ranking in his or her value system. On that basis it becomes possible to accept its mediocrity. Logical lovers are likely to make such statements as, "After all, he *is* a good provider, and that's more important than my having an orgasm every time we make love." . . . "I'd like to have sex more often than we do, but she *is* a good mother and that's what really counts."

Unlike the Romantic lover, who as we shall see is frequently consumed by sexual tension in the presence (or the absence) of the beloved, the Logical lover is able to remain in control of his or her sexual feelings when such control is necessary or desirable. Consider this comment by an attractive woman of thirty-five who teaches at a college in Massachusetts while her husband, an astronomer, works most of the year at an observatory in Arizona.

"I know that people wonder about our sex lives. They probably think I'm having an affair with one of my colleagues, or even sleeping with a student. They don't come right out and say it, but I can see the question in their eyes: How can anybody go so many months without sex? At first I thought it would be prudent not to give any cause for gossip. I arrived at and left dinner parties alone, never accepted even the most casual kind of date. But after a while I realized how foolish I was being. Elliot, my husband, and I trust each other completely. Why should I worry about what other people might think? Besides, while I didn't miss sex I did miss social companionship. So now I do go out with men occasionally, but always with the understanding that it is solely on a platonic basis. Of course, there are times when the physiological tensions build up and I do need release. When that happens, I masturbate. It's quite satisfactory. Then too, the period of abstinence has its own build-in reward. When Elliot and I are together —and we rendezvous frequently at a midway point for a long weekend, or during vacations—our sex life is intensely passionate. We each appreciate the other so much more for having been apart."

Another couple, married for eight years, are separated from each other six months out of twelve because the husband's import-export business requires him to make two lengthy trips each year to the Orient. When we asked how that affected their love relationship both spouses said they find their way of life emotionally and sexually satisfying.

Phillip: I think your question is more peculiar than our way of living. Why is it assumed that two people can be happy only if they are always together? Why is uninterrupted sexual availability so important? For Margery and me, the interplay of absences and reunions makes marriage all the more refreshing.
Margery: Though ten thousand miles are between us, emotionally we are still close. I spend a good deal of time thinking about our life together, planning for the future. Philip does the same. He writes long, thoughtful letters that in many ways help me to understand him better than I can when we talk together. And when he comes home we have so many ideas to exchange. We are fresh to each other each time—not only physically but emotionally and intellectually as well.

But what about sexual jealousy and sexual trust?

Philip: True, Margery is alone for weeks or months at a time. She has ample opportunity for affairs, if she chooses. But I happen to believe she *won't* choose to sleep around because that is not her character. If she were to become involved sexually with another man, I know it would have to be someone special, someone for whom she felt love as well as physical attraction. But that danger would exist even if I never left home.

If sex becomes sufficiently unsatisfactory so that it threatens to outweigh the positive factors or to unbalance the even tenor of a relationship, a Logical lover is likely to examine the situation rationally and take practical steps to remedy it. He or she might consult a marital or sex therapist. Or, like this husband, instead of blaming the other person for the problem, examine whether part of the fault might be his own:

"I didn't realize that my wife and I had a sexual problem," said the thirty-year-old artist, "until I discovered that for two years she had been having an affair with a former lover. When I got over my first shock I asked her why she had done that. She said that I didn't make love to her often enough, didn't even seem interested in sex. 'But you never mentioned anything to me about that!' I said. 'Of course I did, many times," she replied, 'but you usually side-stepped any discussion.' The more I thought about it, the more I realized how right my wife was, and how sexually frustrating our marriage must have been for her.

"I had to confront the question, how much was I to blame for her getting involved with someone else? Gradually, my wife and I began to talk more openly about sex, about what it meant to each of us and how we felt about its importance in our relationship. Though I still experienced sexual desire far less often than my wife did, I realized that if I wanted to preserve my marriage I would have to be more ardent. To my surprise, as I began to make love to her more often I grew more interested in sex myself."

The sexual behavior of the Possessive lover is characterized by extravagant demands and exaggerated anxieties. Possessives have such a great need to be loved that at some level of unconscious awareness they resent the pressure of that need. As a result, their approach to sex is likely to be ambivalent. Possessive lovers seem to place an enormous emphasis on the sexual side of a relationship. More often than not, however, that emphasis may serve as a mask for a lack of sexual self-confidence. One man, a high scorer in the Possessive category, admitted that he never felt certain of a woman's love until he had coaxed, cajoled, importuned, or, finally, coerced her into having sex with him in every possible way, and especially under circumstances where the risk of discovery was high. Only if a woman would go that far, the man said, did he feel she truly "loved" him.

Because they are unable to exert much control over their own emotions, Possessive lovers need to feel they control a partner's emotions. Not surprisingly, then, sexual jealousy is a frequent hallmark of this love style. Jealousy can of course be a valid and normal response to an actual threat to a love relationship. It can also be a totally unrealistic and irrational response, almost a form of paranoia. For most men and women jealousy falls somewhere between these points. It is a suspicion or resentment, perhaps reasonable, perhaps not, of someone (or some *thing*—a demanding job, a consuming hobby) that looms as a rival for a loved one's time and affection. To believe that the one we love may be emotionally close, much less sexually intimate, with another person can arouse deep anxieties. *What if he/she leaves me? What if I am not a good enough lover for him/her?*

Such fears reveal jealousy for what it basically is: a gnawing sense of inadequacy, a lack of self-esteem. But in the Possessive lover jealousy can trigger especially intense reactions. One woman, suspecting that her lover was sleeping with another woman, barraged the man with questions even though she really did not want her suspicions confirmed. When they were, she hurled a costly piece of sculpture through a plate-glass window. In another instance a man who was infatuated with an extraordinarily beautiful woman attempted to make her give up her other suitors and promise to see no one but him. When she refused to do this—"to become one of your possessions," she said, with unconscious insight—he was overcome with jealousy and self-doubt. Partly in revenge, partly to reassure himself, and partly to assert a degree of "control" over the woman, the man telephoned her every midnight to make sure she was at home. If she was out, he envisioned her in bed with another man and spent a sleepless night in jealous self-torment. After a few weeks of phone calls the woman eased his pain, in one sense, by breaking off their relationship.

Most Possessives defend a "reasonable" amount of jealous behavior as a sign of continuing love. Indeed, many men and women, no matter what their love style, view jealousy as a harmless or even stimulating compliment: "It means your partner isn't taking you for granted." According to psychiatrist Dr. Robert Seidenberg, however, it is only when a couple are quite sure of each other's love that they can safely indulge in this sort of playfulness. "Each mate takes turns in accusing the other of infidelity when they are quite sure of their devotion," he writes. "'How come the butcher gives you the best cuts of meat?' he asks. Later she might say, 'No wonder you're so tired at night, with that new blonde secretary at the office.' But when trust is lacking in one or the other partner there is no laughter. Instead there is the serious, 'Just what did you mean by that remark?' The remarks are innocent to those able to love well, but are no joke to those whose hold on reality and to an object are tenuous at best. It is a sign of loyalty when people can share their illicit suspicion fantasies, and a sign of mistrust when everything must be concrete—no playful accusations allowed. . . ."[6]

In some cases a Possessive lover will try to exert emotional or sexual control by reversing the normal flow of jealousy—by trying to make a *partner* jealous. When that happened to Laura, a twenty-five-year-old medical researcher, it took her a while to realize what was happening:

"I'd been going with Mark for almost a year. I liked him a great deal but I wasn't sure I wanted to marry him. Mark never stopped pressuring me, though, and I finally decided I did love him enough to say yes. But once Mark was sure of my feelings his attitude changed. He'd call at the last minute with some patently phony excuse why he couldn't keep our date. He would tell me how he had to brush off the adoring women in his office. Or he'd make a pass at a woman at a party and then look over at me and shrug, as if to say, 'What can I do? She likes me.'

"I was never the jealous type but Mark had me behaving like a first-class bitch. One night we had a big fight about the way he was acting, and I suddenly realized Mark was enjoying every minute of it. He *wanted* me to be jealous. 'What kind of man needs a woman to be jealous of him?' I asked myself. The answer was clear: a man who wasn't sure of himself sexually but who needed to control others that way. When I felt certain I was right, I walked out on Mark for good."

Because of their high level of anxiety, Possessive lovers may have sexual problems that derive from anxiety-related causes, such as vaginismus or premature ejaculation. Vaginismus, an involuntary spasm of pelvic and vaginal muscles that prevents intercourse, is usually an anxiety response. Premature ejaculation, probably the most common male sexual problem, also is closely associated with anxiety. There are many reasons why one may have such a high degree of sexual apprehension, but one of the important ones is a sense of insecurity in the relationship. Possessive lovers are by definition unsure of themselves and jealous of their partners. By their reasoning, love itself does not exist without such feelings. The Possessive's dilemma, however, is that the accompanying tension can also cause sexual dysfunction. Some Possessives love others in spite of the misery they may bring. And some Possessives seem to love others *because* of the misery they can bring.

The Romantic lover is aroused sexually by the sheer fact of being in love, or even by the prospect of being in love. Since a main characteristic of the Romantic style is its quick and intense response to physical appearance and physical attraction, feelings of love are acted out sexually as promptly as circumstances—and the other person—permit. Many Romantics, men and women alike, say they went to bed with their lovers soon after meeting them as a sort of litmus test of whether the partner would measure up sexually to their expectations. In any event a Romantic lover almost always *perceives* sex with the other person as perfect, or certainly capable of becoming perfect, regardless of the realities of the experience. In effect, an erotic circle is created. Romantic love is sparked by physical attraction; physical attraction leads to sexual intimacy; and sexual intimacy reinforces Romantic love.

Research has shown that, in the most basic stages of

sexual excitement, the more physically aroused a person is, the higher he or she rates a partner as attractive and sexually receptive. An emotional affinity based on such arousal may easily be interpreted by a Romantic as the beginnings of love. Caroline had such a definition of love. She and her husband, Bud, met when she was eighteen and he was twenty-one. Now Caroline, at thirty-five, is a home-maker, involved in community affairs and considered conventional by her friends. She is almost embarrassed as she confides that she and Bud had sex on their first date:

"It was in the spring of my freshman year in college. A group of girls went to a dance and Bud walked in with his friends. He was on the football team and I was awe-struck. I never dreamed he would notice me. He asked me to dance and my knees almost buckled. Then he asked if he could take me home and I nearly died with excitement. We parked, and I just knew this time I couldn't resist. I'd done lots of petting with other dates, but never all the way. I even thought that I was probably just another girl to Bud—that turned out to be wrong, fortunately—but I didn't care.

"The next day I was in a daze. I'm not sure how I got through the week until he called. He said he loved me. Imagine! And I thought, 'This *must* be love.' We got married that summer. It hasn't always been easy because at first we didn't know each other well at all. But we've struggled along so far—and sex has always been great. In many ways that has probably held us together even when other things were bad for us."

The Romantic style, which as we pointed out earlier involves a constant search for new ways to please the beloved, also goes to great lengths to keep sex varied and stimulating. Romantics are likely to set aside a special leisurely time for love-making rather than to crowd it in hurriedly at bedtime after a tiring day. Romantics will plan a seductive environment for sex (wine, music, colored lights, incense, satin sheets) or vary its locale (a beach, a meadow, the shower, the hot tub). The Romantic is also playful in his or her sexuality. The composer Frédéric Chopin frequently teased his mistress, Delphine, by referring to her genital area as the "little D flat major," because on the piano keyboard D flat is a black key that lies between two white ones. "Who knows," Chopin wrote, musing on the idea that love-making drains artistic creativity, "what ballades, polonaises, perhaps an entire concerto, have been forever engulfed in your little D flat major?"[7] Chopin also referred to Delphine's sex organ by the musical term "tacit"—which stands for a pause in the music—since, he explained to her, a pause is a hole in the melody.

To prevent love-making itself from falling into a routine, the Romantic will diligently seek out and apply a wide variety of sexual techniques. (But if his or her partner does not have a large amount of the Romantic style as well, this approach may backfire.) And though postcoital melancholy is supposed to be a universal condition, Romantics seem to experience little or none of this sexual sadness. They are more likely to gaze adoringly at the partner, to talk, to touch, to replay in memory every moment of their love-making in order to savor it again.

Some long-married Romantics deliberately try to re-create the glamorous excitement of their earlier sexual encounters by staging a make-believe "affair" or an "illicit" rendezvous with a partner. An example of how the Romantic imagination can work along these lines was provided by the case of Tom, an airline dispatcher, and Irene, a commercial artist. The couple separated after twelve years of marriage and two children when each spouse admitted having recently started an affair. The marital therapist whose help the couple sought soon realized that Tom and Irene were hungry for the stimulation that comes with feeling oneself freshly desired. For while they said the affairs were exciting they admitted there was something synthetic about it all. What Tom and Irene really wanted to experience was the intensity of feeling that had existed in their own earlier romance.

The therapist decided to try an experiment. She instructed the couple to travel separately to a resort hotel, check in individually, and get separate rooms. Each spouse was told to "role-play" from then on as if they were strangers who were suddenly and strongly attracted to each other. At seven o'clock they were to go to the hotel bar, make contact, agree to have dinner together, go dancing, and then let nature take its course. The plan worked. "Our

love-making that evening," Irene said, "was the most exciting in years." For Romantics, at least, keeping sexual love
alive may require little more than a touch of inventiveness
and the willingness to enact a charade they enjoy.

For the Unselfish lover, sex is a comparatively minor
factor. Love is experienced and expressed primarily on
a caring level. The Unselfish lover's main concern is to
meet a partner's needs. If these needs include sex, he or
she will fulfill the need either as a duty done with com-
passion or as a gift given with love. But the Unselfish lover's
own sexual needs or desires are subordinated to those of
the other person.

> "He doesn't thrill me sexually," said a forty-one-year-
> old woman of her husband, "but he loves me and de-
> pends on me. I couldn't possibly leave him. I couldn't
> take a lover. I wouldn't hurt my husband for anything.
> So we have sex when he wants it and I manage to enjoy
> myself most of the time."

While this attitude may puzzle or astound many people,
apparently it is not uncommon in otherwise good marriages. For example, a study by sex therapists at the Western Psychiatric Institute and Clinic of the University of
Pittsburgh reports that good and frequent sex is often not
important in many happy marriages. Even negative feelings
about sex do not change a spouse's positive feelings about
the partner. The only factor that matters, the researchers
reported, is whether both partners are untroubled about sex
they have or don't have. Since a person who defines love in
the Unselfish style wants to meet a partner's needs, the yard-
stick used to measure whether his or her sex life is good
is how satisfied the partner is. As one husband told us: "I
don't think about sex often, but I know my wife wants sex
two or three times a week. So I make it a point to satisfy
her often enough. I'm not sure she even knows I could
go for weeks without sex if it weren't that I want to please
her."

The sexual and emotional welfare of the beloved is far
more important to the Unselfish lover than his or her own
sexual satisfaction. As one observer rather harshly remarked, "This type of lover is more likely to help a partner

get treatment for a venereal disease contracted from some-one else than to be angry about the infidelity." But though Unselfish lovers may often deny their own needs, they should guard against feeling martyred or used. Even for the most giving of lovers, there is a limit.

LOVE STYLES AND INFIDELITIES

There has been a steady increase in infidelity during the past ten years. Mobility, affluence, a constant bombard-ment of sexual stimuli in our environment, a greater social tolerance for sexual experiment—all these have combined to make fidelity not only rarer but more difficult to pre-serve. Therapists who use much of their professional skills untangling clients' love lives seem ready neither to con-demn infidelity nor to recommend it. Most would agree with Dr. Laura Singer, a former president of the American Association for Marital and Family Therapy, who once remarked, "If we are honest with ourselves, we realize that almost everyone, at one time or another, has sexual desires for persons other than his or her spouse. . . . The crucial issue is whether or not we act on those desires." That decision, in turn, depends to a considerable extent on how infidelity fits—or fails to fit—into the emotional patterns of the different styles of love.[8]

A *Best Friend* lover, motivated by mutual trust and loyalty, is unlikely to become involved in an extramarital affair. The necessity for secrecy, for duplicity, is in itself enough of a dissuasion. Yet at the same time the very companionate basis of friendly love can provide a ration-ale for infidelity. A forty-year-old engineer, devoted to his wife in every way, told us:

"I have had relationships with other women. My wife may have had lovers, too. But we both know that they could never cause us to break our primary tie to each other. We are too good friends for that, and no one could ever take her place with me. But sometimes sex with someone else seems to happen naturally. I travel a lot and it's lonely on the road. If an occasional in-fidelity makes me happier, I'll be a better person for my wife to live with. She knows I would never want to share my life with anyone else, and that kind of commitment makes a sexual fling harmless."

We have already seen that a Best Friend lover does not invest sex with overwhelming importance. It is apt to be viewed simply as a natural extension of the closeness one feels with an intimate friend. For this reason, some infidelities experienced by Best Friend lovers are an outgrowth of close friendships they have with others.

"Whoever said you can't share sex with more than one person at a time?" asks Claude, a veteran of thirty-five years of marriage. "My wife and I have a good sex life, and she is the best friend I have in the world. But that doesn't mean that I don't have other good women friends, too. Sometimes sex is a part of the relationship and sometimes it is not. I think we make much too big a fuss about the importance of sex to a relationship. I have felt closer to some of the women I haven't been to bed with than some that I have. None of this has anything to do with how I feel about my wife. We have something together that makes our marriage good even if we couldn't have sex at all. Believe me, it takes a whole lot more than sex to make a marriage work for thirty-five years."

While infidelity is not that frequent, then, for the Best Friend lover, it does occur from time to time. But the sexual double standard may be alive and well for Best Friend lovers, for women seem less apt to be unfaithful than men. It may be that they still are more conventional than men about being sexually disloyal to their best friends.

Conversely, infidelity is often a temptation to both men and women *Game-Playing* lovers. The risk and excitement of an affair can challenge their competitive spirit and stimulate their narcissism. "I know I'm taking a risk of being found out by my husband," one woman said. "But that adds an extra fillip of excitement to the whole thing. Sometimes I look at myself in the mirror and think, 'Imagine, *me* having a lover!' At least he has the same first name as my husband. That way if I talk in my sleep there's no harm done." But Game Players' affairs often end abruptly if the other person becomes too serious or possessive. The affair that spices life at first can become distasteful later if the new lover attempts to tie them down.

Game-Playing lovers' needs for challenge and excitement seem to extend to sex. One man in this category quoted George Bernard Shaw as an example of a kindred soul: "Beauty is all very well, but who ever looks at it when it has been in the house three days?" The Game Player then went on to say: "It's strange how, once I feel really secure with a woman in a loving relationship, my mind starts to wander to what I *don't* have. Excitement is missing when I get to feeling that comfortable." Some experts believe that the search for sexual novelty is built into our biological nature. We do not always give it free rein, they reason, because it is counterbalanced by our need for emotional security. So that, while nearly everyone experiences both urges, there are great individual differences in how we act upon them. Game-Playing lovers clearly have a high need for novelty. Psychologist Marvin Zuckerman has written extensively in this connection about what he calls the "sensation-seeking motive." He developed a scale to measure this personality variable and found that on a day-to-day basis some men and women need more sensation-producing experiences than others. Frequently they find them in sexual encounters.[9]

To the person with a *Romantic* love style infidelity can appear to be an exotic interlude. Susceptible to the physical appeal of a handsome man or beautiful woman, Romantics are frequently led into infidelities by their unrealistic expectations of sexual delights and by the belief that they may be "missing" some incredibly arousing experience. Or if a mate proves not to give the Romantic what he or she needs, it may be sought elsewhere. This should not be too surprising. Today's world is filled with promises of intense sexual pleasures that can make even the best monogamous sexual relationship seem boring, especially to a confirmed Romantic. Others, however, downplay the connection between romance and excitement. They redefine romance. "I thought we had lost romance because sex was no longer as exciting as it used to be," one husband confided. "But after we talked it over my wife and I gradually realized that was only to be expected. After all, we're not honeymooners any more. We realized sex doesn't always have to produce fireworks to be satisfying. Tenderness can be just as romantic if you know enough to appreciate it."

It might seem from our description of the *Unselfish* lover's approach to sex that infidelity would be the last thing one would expect. But the Unselfish lover's Achilles heel is his or her very altruism—the desire to help a troubled person so long as it does not hurt the partner. One woman became involved in an affair with a younger man when he told her he was impotent. "I felt I was mature enough to help him," she said. "I didn't need sex. I needed to take care of *his* need." Here is another instance of the same reasoning:

"I thought I was quite happily married when I first met Judith," said a middle-aged editor. "I had hired her to work on my magazine, and she spent a lot of time in my office telling me the story of her life. Judy had had nothing but trouble! An unhappy childhood, a bad marriage, two disastrous relationships with other men. It was easy to sympathize with Judy—she was sexy, lovely in a fragile sort of way, and she never asked for pity or seemed to pity herself. At any rate, I got caught up in her life.

"I began to think how unfair it was that at the end of the day I had a wife and a comfortable home waiting for me while Judy went back to what I imagined was a cold and empty apartment. It wasn't much of a step from there to believe that if only things were different I might be able to bring her some happiness. On the pretext of needing to discuss her work, I asked Judy to have dinner with me a couple of evenings a week. One night she asked me up to her place for a nightcap, and I accepted. When we were sitting together on the sofa she told me how much I meant to her, how much she needed me. Well, I don't have to tell you we went to bed together then. I didn't feel guilty at all. It didn't seem a bit wrong. I think it would have seemed wrong *not* to give her whatever affection and consolation I could."

A *Logical* lover usually considers it foolish to risk a basically rewarding relationship for the more intense but impractical pleasures of infidelity. Yet the Logical love style also implies that if marital sex is unfulfilling it is reasonable to seek other avenues of satisfaction. The practical lover may thus take another sexual partner if he or she decides it "makes sense" to do so. Unlike the Game Player, who may be unfaithful out of the desire to win another sexual contest, the Logical lover may take another sexual partner in order to better sustain a relationship with his or her primary partner. For example:

"My marriage is good in every way save one," says a vigorous and vital fifty-five-year-old attorney. "Mary is a wonderful wife, a wonderful person. Except for her lack of interest in sex she is all that any man could want. In the early years of our marriage she tried to overcome her sexual reluctance, and I tried to overlook it. But now she doesn't even try to pretend any more. She takes the position that a woman over fifty is finished with the sexual part of life. If that distresses me, she says, then I should consider myself free to do whatever I want.

"Well, the idea of casual infidelities never appealed to me. As a lawyer, I've seen too many marriages destroyed by them. But I faced a dilemma. I wasn't ready to give up sex, yet I did not want to humiliate my wife or risk our marriage. I solved the problem by instigating a sensible low-key affair with a woman I met at a legal conference. She's thirty-eight, divorced for a long time, has no children. I told her the truth: that I was attracted to her physically, that sex at home was non-existent, and that while I wanted to be with her as much as possible there was no question of the relationship going beyond that stage.

"Somewhat to my surprise, she was more than willing. I guess our love affair fills a gap in her life, too. Our affair is in its second year now. We manage it most discreetly, so that my marriage has not been disrupted. My wife may suspect what I'm doing, but she asks no questions. She is probably relieved that the one area of conflict between us no longer corrodes the rest of our time together."

We already know that the *Possessive* lover is jealous—even obsessed by the thought that the loved one might stray. He or she is usually so engrossed in the relationship that the idea of wanting to have a sexual relationship with anyone else seems unthinkable. But the Possessive lover is not generally guided by logic or rationality. The fact is that Possessives frequently stray into or deliberately seek out affairs for revenge, or to make the partner jealous, or to salve a wounded ego. Their affairs are more apt to be reactions than actions. Consider, for example, the re-action of a middle-aged executive whose wife cancelled a trip with him because of pressures in her own job. The man at first accused her of caring more about her work than she did about him, but then escalated his jealousy until he was convinced that what his wife really cared more for was her boss. Consumed with hurt and fury, the man invited a woman acquaintance to go with him on the trip. His ego was enhanced, and he felt it served his wife right.

The Possessive lover may think nothing of making enormous emotional demands on a partner and, if they are not met, punishing him or her by being unfaithful. Thus when one man's fiancée behaved in what he considered an aloof and unloving way, he immediately telephoned a former lover and restarted their affair. He had to feel re-assured that *someone* cared for him.

Possessive lovers also are often extremely dependent. But, like a teen-ager who begins to resent being dependent on parents, the Possessive needs to make occasional at-tempts at independence, to show a partner that "I can do without you." An infidelity often serves—or seems to serve —this purpose:

Lucille was married to a prominent and handsome sur-geon. He got so much attention from women patients and nurses that Lucille was in an almost constant state of jealousy. When she confessed her fears her husband would smile, pat her on the fanny, and tell her how foolish she was being. And because she was dependent, Lucille did try to forget her suspicions. One day, how-ever, after a particularly violent scene, the surgeon stamped out of the house. "Since you're already con-vinced I'm unfaithful," he said, "maybe I *will* be." "Show him!" a well-meaning woman friend of Lucille's said. "Find your own lover." Egged on this way, Lucille encouraged the already more than friendly attitude of her son's tennis teacher. Soon they were sleeping together. But now Lucille is jealous of the lithe women who take tennis lessons from her lover. In attempting to break her emotional dependency on her husband, Lucille has succeeded only in transferring it to another man.

8

PARTNERSHIP COMBINATIONS: MATCHES AND MISMATCHES

What is irritating about love is that it . . . requires an accomplice.

—Baudelaire

. . . these are the people who pass their whole lives together; yet they could not explain what they desire of one another.

—Plato, *Symposium*

It is Christmas Eve. A young engaged couple raise glasses of champagne to toast each other and their approaching marriage. They exchange gifts. "Open yours first," he says. She lifts away the tissue paper and gasps in delight as the gold and jade bracelet reveals itself to her. "It's beautiful!" she says. "It's just what I wanted! How did you know?"

"Remember when we went shopping for a wedding ring last month?" he says. "I saw how this bracelet attracted you. You asked the clerk to let you try it on, and when you gave it back to him you took it from your wrist so-o-o reluctantly. Even anyone who *didn't* love you would know how much you liked it."

She kisses him and then, with a small anticipatory smile of triumph, says, "Now yours." He takes the package, attacks the wrappings, opens the box, and stares at his gift. He recognizes it instantly—the loose-fitting sweater jacket with its fashionable bulky shawl collar which for months she has been after him to buy even though, rightly or wrongly, he feels he looks ridiculous in it. He wonders how to react. Should he repress his irritation and pretend to be pleased?

"I know you kept telling me you didn't want one," she says, carefully gauging the expression on his face. "But you'll really enjoy wearing it once you get used to it."

A warning note sounds in his mind. He knows that the presents lovers give each other often reveal a good deal of how they think and feel about the relationship. He, Romantically and Unselfishly, has given her exactly what he knew she wanted. She, Possessively, has asserted her need to control him by giving him exactly what she wanted him to want.

A minor matter? Perhaps. Sooner or later the incident may be overlooked, forgiven, allowed to fade in memory. On the other hand it may foreshadow a continuing series of such occurrences. In any event it is certainly a cautionary signal—a clear warning that this couple's individual styles of love may not be well matched.

There is as yet little research that can tell us whether partners with similar definitions of love are likely to have more stable or more satisfying relationships than partners with differing definitions. You will recall that two major theories of marital choice which suggest that we are attracted either to someone very much like ourselves or to someone temperamentally different from us—provided that those differences complement one another. In a sense these patterns also hold true for love-style partnerships. Two people whose ways of loving are alike can reinforce each other emotionally because they empathize with each other's feelings so well. Since we tend to love as we ourselves want to be loved, this mutuality enhances the relationship. And a couple whose styles of loving are *not* the same, but nevertheless mesh in emotionally significant ways, can also have a rewarding partnership.

The key factor is not whether styles are similar or different but whether they are compatible with each other. It is reasonable to expect, for example, that some unions of same-style partners would be much more satisfying than others. A man and woman who are both primarily Logical in their approach to love could be expected to get along well (although others may feel their lack of spontaneity is boring). Yet in other instances sameness may work against a couple. It can generate an emotionally destructive relationship if, say, two Possessives are involved; or, if both persons have a Best Friend love style, a relationship that may be excessively bland. Actress Liv Ullman, talking of her divorce, says that when she and her husband went to a marriage counselor's office they sat side by side and held hands. "The counselor asked why we wished to separate if we were such good friends," recalls the actress. " 'Just for that reason,' we replied cheerfully."[1]

By the same token, some pairings of partners with differing love styles work out well while others seem ready made for the hazards of frustration, loneliness, and emotional pain. One of the most happily married couples we spoke with say they feel lucky to have kept their love alive while so many of their friends are divorcing. "What seems to make the difference," Eleanor said, "is that Jim and I manage to bridge our differences instead of letting them alienate us." According to their Love Scale scores, Jim combines Best Friend and Romantic styles while Eleanor is chiefly Logical and Unselfish. As might be predicted, Jim's romanticism and Eleanor's practicality have clashed from time to time. On occasion he wishes she were more sexual and sentimental; she is sometimes impatient with his penchant for "wasting" money on gifts and celebrations. But the Unselfish quality of Eleanor's love helps her to accept Jim's romanticism without too much fuss. And his Best Friend aspect makes him genuinely concerned for her happiness. Despite the contrast in their definitions, this couple's love flourishes because their styles are compatible and because they respect each other's right to be different.

Difficulties are more likely to occur when styles diverge more widely and conflict more acutely, so that the partners' ways of expressing love are considerably at odds. For instance, when a young husband complained that his Logical and Unselfish wife was not sufficiently affectionate, she responded by trying to be more openly romantic and more sexually assertive as a sign of her love. But these sudden overtures were too overpowering and threatening for her Game-Playing husband. Terrified at the prospect of her willingness to make this kind of commitment to him, he became impotent.

Many of the common irritants in close relationships frequently stem from unrecognized differences in love styles. We listened recently to a group of couples—some married, some living together—talk about the tensions they feel when one person's desire for privacy clashes with the other's desire for closeness. "My wife complains that I always go into another room to read," a man said. "Believe me, I would if I could, but she follows me wherever I go. If I want to take a walk, *she* wants to walk. If I decide to work in the garden, *she* decides to work in the garden too." A woman in the group declared, "It's gotten to the point where I have to get in the car and drive around the streets if I want to be alone." The chances are that in each of these situations the partner seeking a bit of privacy has a good deal of the Best Friend love style in his or her make-up. Temporary separation is no threat to such a person, merely part of the normal ebb and flow of togetherness and separateness he or she considers a normal part of loving behavior. The other partner, however, has the earmarks of a Possessive or a Romantic. In another case a woman considered postponing her imminent wedding because, she said, she could not understand how her fiancé could love her when he argued with her all the time. "He gets furious one minute, and the next minute he acts as if nothing happened between us," she said. "How can I believe he really cares about me?" To this woman's Romantic concept, love was not love unless it was all sweetness and light. To the man's Best Friend approach, there was no reason to think that a good argument implied an absence of love. Indeed, he could not feel comfortable arguing with anyone he did not care about deeply. Nor could he feel secure in his love unless he could express his disagreement.

In theory it is possible for a partnership between any set of styles to produce some degree of emotional distress. That is true even for a couple who are both high in Unselfish love. Such a union might be thought immune to misunderstandings, yet consider the story of Barbara and John. She works at a job she hates because she thinks the couple need her salary to make ends meet. John inwardly dislikes the idea of Barbara's working, yet he suppresses his personal preference because he believes Barbara feels the job is important to her sense of independence. They are heading for conflict because each is unselfishly hiding true feelings out of concern for what both assume is the other person's needs.

PARTNERSHIP COMBINATIONS: MATCHES

Although there is no way of guaranteeing that any pairing of styles will work better than any other (or will work at all), experience does show that certain combinations tend to result in harmonious matches. Best Friend partnerships—where both persons rank high in that category— seem to produce enduring and loving relationships. These are the couples who can live together in an isolated cabin in the woods or travel together on a six-month freighter cruise without becoming bored or irritated by each other. Here is how one wife describes such a marriage:

> "My husband and I are quite different in many outward respects—family background, religion, age—but that does not interfere with the inner serenity we feel. We are decidedly each other's good friend. Both of us shy away from emotional outbursts, and we probably would not qualify as exciting lovers. Our marriage probably seems awfully low-key to other people, perhaps even dull and uninspiring. But it is steady and solid. Before we were married we sometimes had to adopt different attitudes in order to appear 'sexy' enough to attract other people. But when we met each other we were relieved and delighted to be able to be ourselves."

As we have said, no one has a totally "pure" love style. The mixtures that seem to combine most effectively with a Best Friend style include the Romantic, the Logical, and the Unselfish. Some well-known couples who exemplify those kinds of partnerships might include former President Gerald Ford and his wife, Betty, and Henry and Nancy Kissinger. The diplomat had been divorced for ten years when he met his wife-to-be during the hurly-burly of the Republican National Convention in 1964. "I fell in love with her the moment I met her," Kissinger has been quoted as saying, "but it took me two years to tell her so." Nancy required twice as long to reach her decision: "I take things too seriously to believe in love at first sight," she has said. "Quick decisions aren't part of my personality." From the evidence, the Kissingers' relationship would seem to be a partnership between a Best Friend/Romantic man and a Best Friend/Logical woman. "We are very close," Kissinger has said. "I don't know if that's romantic or not, but Nancy is a marvelous balance wheel."[2]

The Fords seem to be a good illustration of a Best Friend partnership with touches of the Romantic and Unselfish in Betty's style and a substantial amount of Logical in her husband's. While she knew quite soon after dating Gerald Ford that she wanted to marry him, he postponed his decision until he had good reason to feel that he would be elected to Congress. (Even on his wedding day Ford campaigned until moments before the ceremony.) The sacrifices Mrs. Ford made for the sake of her husband's political career have been well documented. Even though living up to the requirements of being a legislator's wife caused Mrs. Ford considerable emotional and physical stress— when Ford was Minority Leader of the House of Representatives he was away from her and their four children for 258 days in one year—she was still able to say: "I married Jerry because I loved him, and I was willing to put up with his being away from home." (Another First Lady, Pat Nixon, once said: "I have sacrificed everything in my life that I consider precious in order to advance the career of my husband." Perhaps anyone who plans to be in public or political life would do well to make sure his or her partner rates high in the Unselfish style of love.)

But that kind of Best Friend/Unselfish combination is just as effective for ordinary couples. Gretchen and Steve were neighbors who became close friends after their respective spouses ran away together:

"Steve and I were blind to what was going on right under our noses," Gretchen said. "I remember once, after we saw our mates hugging and kissing, we talked almost kiddingly about what might be happening. Steve said he thought they had a little too much to drink. So you can imagine our shock when they told us they were filing for divorce so they could marry each other.

"They left that very night. Steve and I literally held each other together for several months. I helped him with his children and his housework. He repaired things for me and took my boys to their Little League games. I cooked for all of us and Steve helped buy groceries. One night, exactly five months after our ex-es had left, Steve put his arms around me and kissed me. It was partly symbolic for both of us of our mutual sharing and respect. But we had also come to know that we loved each other."

A partnership between predominantly Logical lovers is also frequently successful. They tend to choose each other after careful thought and continue to map out their lives in an orderly fashion, much like the scientists Pierre and Marie Curie; his proposal of marriage included an invitation to share a life of scientific discovery that would "benefit the world." Over the years we have watched many graduate students follow this pattern. Drawn together by common interests, their collaboration on research projects often leads to emotional relationships and then to marriage. Lauren and Tracy offer a classic example of how two such Logical lovers are attracted to each other and how they organize their lives. The couple met three years ago in graduate school (each has a doctorate in psychology), found teaching positions in the same community, and shared an apartment for six months to test how they got along before deciding to marry. Lauren is now pregnant. "We planned things so the baby will be born in June, when I finish teaching," she says. "That also means I have three months before the fall semester in which to give the baby a good start with breast feeding." Lauren and Tracy have already begun interviewing prospective baby sitters! In an era when the two-career family is increasingly common, a match between Logical lovers evidently has much to recommend it.

In ordinary circumstances a partnership between two Game-Playing lovers would seem to be risky. Their tendency to seek changing and challenging outside relationships does not augur well for permanence. But for a couple who sincerely believe in—and can sustain—the concept of an "open" marriage, a Game-Playing love style may well function effectively. We talked with one such couple, Gloria and Martin, whose Love Scale profiles show each of them with high scores in Game Playing and medium scores in Logical love styles. In virtually all respects save one the couple have led conventional lives and had a conventional marriage. Both middle-class Midwesterners, Gloria and Martin met in college, married after graduation, raised three children, and are now the proud grandparents of four girls. Yet during all the thirty-three years of their marriage they have had—and still have—occasional love affairs with other partners.

"There were dire predictions for our marriage from the start," Gloria told us. "When the years kept passing and

Martin and I were still devotedly together, people warned that our children would surely show the effects of our way of life and love. But the children have turned out splendidly, and they are close to us. I think the main reason is we have always maintained that if a couple respect their primary commitment to each other, and truly care about each other's welfare, extramarital liaisons don't really matter."

Gloria and Martin resist labeling their marriage an "open" one. "That sounds as if we are part of a fad," Martin argues. "We are simply realists who from the beginning vowed that our marriage would never make either of us feel trapped. We decided this long before the 'open marriage' concept was put forward. We hear other couples who speak of 'giving up their freedom' or of taking on a 'ball and chain' when they get married. Neither of us wanted to feel that way, and we have managed to avoid it very nicely."

Gloria and Martin established and scrupulously observed specific rules for their Game Playing. First, they have always been honest with each other about their outside liaisons. They have agreed that any extramarital relationship—whether or not it involved sex—which seemed to be getting emotionally serious would be promptly ended. "Any intimate friend either of us has must understand and accept from the outset how I feel about Martin and how he feels about me," says Gloria. "This may not be necessary with more casual relationships but it is crucial with long-term or sexual ones." Men are usually shocked when they learn that Gloria's husband knows what she is doing. "One man said I had ruined all his pleasure," Gloria recalls. "He could not respond to me after hearing that."

Over the years Martin and Gloria have met only two or three other couples with similar marriages. "Most of the men and women who seek extramarital affairs are either running from their spouses or deceiving them," Martin says. "It is rare to find two people who not only agree on this style of loving but are both secure enough about themselves and their relationship to carry it off successfully. I don't think either Gloria or I could have survived a marriage with someone who didn't agree that loving is not the same thing as possessing."

PARTNERSHIP COMBINATIONS: MISMATCHES

What are the love-style partnerships most likely to result
in mismatches?[3] As we shall see, there are styles which do
not combine well with *any* other, even the identical one.
What is lacking for each partner is too important, too pervasive, to give up. We have focused, however, on those
pairings which occur with some frequency yet which, research indicates, risk encountering serious emotional stress.
(Though no individual has an unmixed style, we have, for
the sake of clarity, identified the following combinations
by the name of the style which predominates in each partner and gives the relationship its special kind of interaction.)

Ellen's approach to love was thoroughly Romantic. She
had been "in love" more times than she could remember.
But most of those relationships had foundered rather
quickly. Sometimes Ellen fell "out of love" and moved
on to another man. Sometimes it was the man who broke
off the affair. When Ellen met Joel at a party she was not
involved with anyone else. Besides, she thought he was the
handsomest man she had ever seen:

> "Something told me he was going to be Mr. Right,"
> Ellen said. "I think the fact that I was so obviously at-
> tracted to him flattered Joel's ego—and believe me, I
> know now what a huge ego he has. Yet that first night
> he didn't talk about himself at all. He concentrated on
> me. He asked dozens of questions—about my job, my
> parents, where I lived, what kind of car I drove. I had
> never met a man who seemed so genuinely interested
> in me."

But Joel had a Logical love style; he was not asking all
those questions out of idle curiosity. Though Logical lovers
have many good qualities—they are industrious, reliable,
sensible—they tend to be single-minded in their pursuit of
a partner who will further their own goals in life. As Joel
explained:

> "I married Ellen mainly because she was bright, attrac-
> tive, and seemed to have a level head on her shoulders.
> She had a good job and invested her savings wisely. She

even drove a practical car. You see, I have planned my future quite carefully. I expect to be the head of the company I'm with by the time I'm forty years old. I knew all along that the woman I fell in love with and married would have to be an asset to me in that plan. And I thought Ellen had it all. I was excited about the kind of life we could share."

So was Ellen:

"I was enchanted from that very first evening. And it drove me crazy when Joel went about courting me in such a methodical way. At first he would only date me once a week. He said it was important for us not to rush into things, to get to know each other slowly. And I nearly died before we even went to bed with each other. But he insisted on waiting until, as he said, we could do it 'properly.' That meant waiting until he had time to take me away for a long weekend. Of course, it was all planned to perfection. I thought he was being terribly romantic, but now I realize that wasn't it at all. It was just Joel's way of doing things.

"He plans everything in our lives. Nothing is spontaneous. And shortly after we were married he began to plan *my* life too. He wanted me to do all sorts of things that didn't interest me at all—entertain his bosses, go with him to business conventions, and be nice to the bosses' wives. He tried to get me to read certain books he said would improve my mind. I began to feel like a box on Joel's organization chart rather than someone he loved. For a while I went along with all of it, hoping he would change. I mean, it didn't matter to me if Joel got to be president of his company or not. I would have loved him just the same. But he didn't change, and I just couldn't go on doing all those things he wanted me to do. That wasn't my idea of a marriage."

Like a typical Logical lover, Joel took Ellen's refusal to go along with his plans and expectations as a sign that she did not really care about him; if Ellen did not share his approach to their future together, or could not meet his needs, then there must be something fundamentally wrong with their marriage. Otherwise, why would she renege on their "deal"? As an outgrowth of doubting Ellen's love for him, Joel came to doubt his love for her. Naturally, he sought to explain that reaction in Logical terms:

> "I think I have simply outgrown Ellen. She has a good mind, but I don't think she uses it any more. And she has let her appearance go to the point where I am embarrassed to take her to company functions. Nor is she interested in entertaining my colleagues, or joining in the activities of some of the other wives. We simply don't have anything in common any more."

To which Ellen replied:

> "I'll say we don't. Not even sex—and that used to be so good. That's Joel's fault. When I wouldn't go along with his suggestions he would ignore me sexually for weeks at a time. And he knows how important touching and sex are to me. He was using it to punish me. When I'm unhappy I start eating candy and snacks and stuff. The more unhappy I get, the more I eat. I can't help it. And now look at me! But what's the difference? Joel has no sense of romance. I don't think he ever loved me the way I loved him. He just wanted an attractive assistant to help him in his career. Right now I feel as if I'm withering away."

Marital therapy did not help this couple. They both felt too cheated. Ellen's belief that she had found a romantic, caring man—when, in fact, Joel was checking out her qualifications—was wrecked in disillusionment. Joel's belief that he had found a career asset was dashed by Ellen's romantic needs and subsequent decline into apathy when she was disappointed.

Not all Logical lovers give up as quickly as Joel did. Some make an effort to stay with a Romantic partner, to do everything possible to cling to what they have rather than to face an uncertain future. In the effort to balance the scales of love, a Logical lover will often work diligently to make the rewards match the costs. But when the scales continue to tip too heavily on the cost side, they will, also logically, cut their losses. Take Sally as an example. She was originally attracted to her Romantic partner because she had looked a long time for the "right man":

"Both had everything I wanted. But after we'd been married only a few years I discovered he was having affairs. I was terribly hurt, but I wasn't about to give him up to some woman whose only qualification was being good in bed. When I confronted Bob with what I knew he was properly contrite. He said he had gotten involved with other women only because he needed excitement and romance in his life—not because he cared about them, or because he didn't love me.

"So I made up my mind that, if Bob wanted excitement and romance, that's what I would give him. I did everything I could think of to keep him happy sexually. He never knew what I was going to surprise him with next. That worked for a while, and maybe it would have kept on working. But I finally realized that in a sense I was prostituting myself to save my marriage. How's that for irony? I was catering to Bob's needs at a terrible high cost to my self-respect. And when I re-evaluated our relationship in *that* light, I decided that keeping Bob was no longer worth the effort."

A partnership between a Romantic lover and a Best Friend lover can encounter difficulties if the former grows upset when his or her more intense way of loving is met largely by a calmer response. One such couple sought help when the woman interpreted her husband's actions to mean he was falling out of love with her—since by *her* definition he was certainly no longer "in" love with her. Here is how one session in the counselor's office progressed:

Husband: Of course I love my wife. *In* love? I'm not sure just what Marian means by that. Is that different from just plain loving?
Marcia Lasswell: To some people it is. I'm sure your wife thinks it is. *(Turning to woman.)* Have you tried to explain to him what you mean by that?
Wife: A hundred times. When we were first married Ray used to call me from the office once or twice every day, just to tell me he was thinking about me. Many times he'd bring flowers home, or surprise me with an unexpected evening out. But now . . . nothing like that ever happens. He used to like it when I served dinner by candlelight. Now he complains he can't see what he's eating!
Husband: What's more important as a way of showing love

—bringing home flowers or being there when you need me?

As further counseling sessions made clear, Ray essentially had a Best Friend love style. He had *played* the Romantic role during the couple's courtship and early married years, he said, because his wife responded to it so eagerly. In short, Ray had intuitively made the effort to live up to Marian's concept of love. But now he had reverted to his own. Sending birthday or Valentine's Day cards was not important to him. He considered that he was showing love in more "appropriate" ways—working steadily, being sexually faithful, sharing his thoughts with her. It was necessary to help Ray and Marian learn to show their love in ways which the other person considered loving.

A more unusual conflict, this one involving sexual differences between Romantic and Best Friend love styles, plagued the marriage of Sam and Edie:

"About two years ago," says the therapist who dealt with the couple's problem, "Sam, twenty-five, and Edie, twenty-three, came to my office for help. In their two years of marriage they had actually completed sexual intercourse only once. My questions revealed, however, that in the year and a half before their wedding they had spent almost every weekend together and had made frequent and thoroughly satisfying love each time. On their wedding night Edie pleaded exhaustion. Much to Sam's surprise, she continued to refuse intercourse during the entire honeymoon. The night they moved into their own apartment Edie yielded to Sam's insistence but complained of pain during intercourse. By the time I saw the couple they had been to a physician who diagnosed Edie's problem as vaginismus and recommended sex therapy. Edie flatly rejected that idea, and Sam was on the verge of filing for divorce.

"I asked the couple to take the Love Scale Questionnaire. Edie's predominant style was Romantic with a moderate amount of Possessiveness. Sam was a mixture of the Unselfish and Best Friend styles. In our meetings, Edie disclosed that she was an only child and had never seen her parents engage in any behavior or conversation that was sexual in nature. Moreover, when Edie was a teenager her mother had warned her against showing any 'inappropriate' affection toward her father. In high school and college, however, Edie learned from her peers that being affectionate and even having sex was quite acceptable behavior before marriage.

"In short, Edie's basic Romantic concept of love—with all of its sexual urgency—was in direct conflict with her deeply ingrained sentiment that intercourse was appropriate for non-marital relationships but was taboo within a family setting! She was unable to be sexually 'in love' with a husband, since he was a family member. Sam had no such problems. Sex, for him, was a secondary aspect of love and quite appropriate in a family setting. His definition of love as a friendly and unselfish emotion was probably all that kept him in the marriage this long. Edie was willing to accept my analysis of the situation and agreed to try sex therapy. Fortunately, it succeeded."

Another troublesome combination can occur when a Romantic links up with another Romantic. Literature is filled with bittersweet tales of "star-crossed" lovers—Lancelot and Guinevere, Faust and Marguerite, and, of course, Romeo and Juliet. But the fault, as Shakespeare noted in a different context, was not in their stars but in themselves. What often attracts Romantics to each other in the first place may ultimately become the cause of their downfall. Many such pairs are drawn together by an egoistic need to find an extension of their own romantic identities. Others are mutually attracted by the drama of romance that both need. Still others labor at love in order to shape reality into a romantic mold. Moreover, since Romantics tend to fall in love "at first sight," they have little time to learn about each other, or even to assess the circumstances that drew them together. As the "real" other person emerges, it may take not only determination but a strong imagination as well to keep that reality camouflaged in the gossamer of romanticism.

The essential chink in the Romantic's armor is the need to idealize the loved one, no matter what; to see Stendhal's sparkling crystals on the plain bough even when they are *not* there. If a partner turns out to be something else than one hoped or believed, the Romantic nevertheless continues to fashion him or her in that image. Unlike Logicals such as Joel, who cut their losses, Romantics do not easily give up their emotional investment even when love is gone. But idealization cannot go on indefinitely, and the relationship begins to deteriorate when reality sets in. Thus two Romantic partners may well fight a losing battle with time and the exigencies of daily living. Disenchantment leads to disappointment. Studies show that a relationship based solely on Romantic love styles has a life expectancy of less than three years. It either grows to include other dimensions of love, or it disintegrates. In the latter case, each partner begins to feel he or she has erred in choosing the other. Both may deny that what they felt was ever "really" love. They make frequent defensive statements to justify the passion that has cooled: "It was only an infatuation." . . . "I wasn't myself when we met." . . . "I was too young to know what love means." However, true Romantics are likely to do the same thing the next time. They cannot help believing, on a deep emotional level, that it's the only way to fall in love.

While a partnership between a Romantic and a Game Player may not develop into a mismatch, the Game Player's aversion to commitment can present problems:

"I wanted nothing more than a close, loving marriage," one woman said. "But a year or so after Steve and I married he began to avoid my efforts to maintain that kind of contact. Sometimes, when I persisted, he would tease me. I remember once, desperate for some sense of closeness, I said to Steve, 'Talk to me, just talk to me.' He looked at me coolly and said, 'Okay, what do you want to talk about? Give me a topic.' Later, I found Steve was having affairs with two other women. When I told him what I knew he casually admitted that my facts were correct. But, he said, the other women didn't mean anything to him. I couldn't understand that. To me, making love meant you were *in* love.

"For a while I made a fool of myself. I bought provocative clothes I thought would make me look sexier. I changed the color and style of my hair. Steve noticed and complimented me on my new appearance, but it didn't change his attitude. Finally, I decided it was a hopeless situation—not just because Steve did not love me the way I needed to be loved, but because he was incapable of loving *anyone* in a committed way. I told him I wanted a divorce and asked him to move out of the house. Steve seemed almost relieved. It was as if I had lifted a burden from him that he did not know how to lift himself. I helped him pack some of his things and drove him to a small apartment he'd rented. When I turned to say good-by, I began to cry. But not Steve. He put his arm around me and said, 'It's not your fault. If I met you tomorrow for the first time I'd be attracted to you all over again.' I was crying, and he was still playing games."

Men and women with high Possessive love-style scores find it hard to work out satisfactory partnerships with any of the other styles, with the possible exception of an Unselfish lover. It is, of course, theoretically possible for possessiveness to be modified, but that requires a special kind of partner—one who can survive emotional upheavals, is capable of intense feelings, and who can ultimately assuage a Possessive's fear of being *un*loved.

A Possessive in a partnership with a Game Player is likely to be in for a particularly difficult time. One of the more miserable young women we have ever encountered in our counseling office came to seek help for her depression. Maya's love affair with Ted—"the most wonderful, special man" she'd ever met—was not going well at all. In fact it appeared to be over.

In the beginning, Maya told us, Ted could not seem to see enough of her. On days when they could not meet he telephoned her several times just to "hear her voice." He encouraged Maya to share with him her innermost thoughts and feelings; she hardly noticed that Ted rarely talked about himself. Most wonderful of all, Maya was having orgasms. She had never been orgasmic before but Ted "cured" that, she said, with exquisite patience and with his obvious delight in her body. Maya, feeling truly cherished, began to fantasize a lifelong love with Ted. She gave up other men friends and thought of herself as committed to Ted. She moved out of her old apartment and into one closer to his. When Ted had to be out of town on business Maya was miserable; to cheer herself up and feel she was important to him, she cleaned his apartment and stocked the refrigerator with food she knew he liked. For

Maya, everything revolved around Ted. She was totally dependent on him for her happiness.

But true to form for the Game-Playing lover, Ted grew increasingly wary and elusive. He began to push Maya away emotionally. He told her she was "smothering" him with her attentions. He pointed out a host of minor faults in Maya which, he said, bothered her more than he could explain. Though Maya's full figure had at first been an attraction for Ted, he now accused her of letting herself get "fat." The tone of her voice, which once intrigued him, had become grating. He began to break dates at the last minute, pleading work or illness. But the more Ted pulled away to preserve his emotional distance, the more dependent and demanding Maya grew. It was as if she no longer had a sense of her separate self. Ted used her dependency as an excuse to break away for good. "I can't be for you what you want me to be," he told Maya. "It's better that I get out of your life completely."

A match between Possessive and Best Friend styles presents problems of a different kind. For one thing, the friendly love style emphasizes a comfortable, easy relationship. It does not take kindly to the *Sturm und Drang* atmosphere which a Possessive's demanding attitude creates:

"My wife recently had to go away for a few days to take care of her widowed father, who had been in an accident. When she got back she asked if I had missed her. Well, I suppose I did in a way, but after all she wasn't gone forever. And 'missing' isn't part of my style. I told my wife that it had been a little lonely without her but that I had gotten an awful lot done around the house. To my astonishment she flew into a fury. 'If you really loved me,' she said, 'you would have missed me terribly.' That just doesn't make sense to me."

The Possessive lover, trapped in his or her own definition of love, can only interpret such a casual approach to separation as a clear sign of indifference of rejection. The partner is baffled by this reaction. Each misreads the signals the other is sending. Jealousy is another area where signals are likely to be misread. A Possessive lover will actually be distressed if a partner shows no signs of jealousy in what the Possessive considers a provocative situation. Some men and women go out of their way to make a partner jealous. When he or she fails to respond in the "proper" way, the Possessive can only interpret that, too, as a sign of disinterest, a lack of love. "But jealousy isn't love," says the Best Friend lover, "it's a form of neuroticism." "If you really loved me," counters the Possessive, "you'd be distraught at the thought of me with someone else." And means it. If the circumstances were reversed and the Possessive had a real or fancied reason to feel jealous, he or she would be quick to seek revenge and cherish anger.

One couple broke up when the woman could no longer tolerate her lover's jealousy. He was so Possessive that he checked the mileage on her car every day to see if the distance she traveled jibed with the account of her activities he demanded—and she reluctantly gave. After their separation the woman tried to keep in touch with her ex-lover to make sure he was getting along all right. But she could not cope with his coldness. "Why can't we be friends now?" she asked. "Friends?" the man replied. "I can't be friends with you after I've been in love with you, after I've made love to you. I never want you to call me again."

A relationship between two Possessive lovers is likely to provide enough melodrama for the plot lines of several Italian operas. Since Possessives tend to oscillate between peaks of excitement and depths of disappointment, there is the distinct possibility that one partner will be emotionally up at the same time the other is emotionally down. That can be damaging enough to a relationship; but if the couple's highs and lows happen to coincide, each will tend to reinforce the most unpleasant aspects of the other. One of the most revealing portraits of the torture two Possessives can put each other through was drawn by author Sheilah Graham in her autobiography, *Beloved Infidel.* Much of the book is given to recounting her long love affair with F. Scott Fitzgerald when he worked as a scenarist in Hollywood. Because each was insanely jealous of the other they lived together as virtual recluses, often neglecting important work in order to meet each other's emotional demands. At one point in the book Graham describes how she wanted to lose herself in Fitzgerald—"to crawl into his head"[4]—in order to merge their beings into one. After one of Fitzgerald's recurrent bouts with alcoholism she carried out a threat to leave him. He threatened to kill her unless she returned, and taunted her by publicly revealing her real name, about which she was extremely sensitive. She responded by tearing up the first editions of his books, which he had inscribed to her. Each was willing to hurt the other fiercely in the name of Possessive love.

The possible exception to these gloomy prognoses for love relationships with a Possessive is, as we mentioned earlier, the partnership between Possessive and Unselfish styles. A totally giving man or woman who will go to great lengths to understand and accept a Possessive's behavior is best equipped to cope with that manic-depressive approach to love. Even then problems may arise, usually of the Possessive's own making. A woman with high Love Scale scores in both the Possessive and Romantic categories was convinced she no longer loved her husband. Since a major criterion for her definition of love was erotic attraction and response, the fact that the sexual side of her marriage was no longer exciting was evidence enough for the woman that the relationship was dying—even though her husband tried everything he knew to keep their sex life alive. When she met a man with whom she once again experienced sexual passion, she "knew" that she had found "real" love once again. The woman struggled with her conflicting desires: on the one hand marriage, with its claims on her loyalty and its guarantee of security; on the other, her affair and erotic renewal. The stressful situation might have gone on indefinitely had it not been for the Unselfish concern of her husband. He offered her a divorce—"if that would make you happy"—and she accepted.

But some men and women in mismatched partnerships can learn to modify their own love styles—and to understand the other person's—at least enough to move gradually toward emotional compatibility. Natalie and Victor were a potentially mismatched couple who worked out their conflict with the help of a counselor. Both in their mid-thirties, they had been wed a little less than two years when Victor stunned Natalie by saying he thought they should dissolve their marriage. She had no inkling of why he would want to do that, Natalie tearfully told the therapist. In fact, she said, Victor himself could not give her a satisfactory explanation. He was, however, willing to discuss the situation. With both spouses present, the counselor opened their session by getting directly to the main issue:

Marcia Lasswell: Vic, I understand you want a divorce and Natalie doesn't. She says you won't discuss your reasons. Is this true?

Vic: No. I've told her all there is to tell. *(Calmly.)* I just don't love her any more.

M.L.: When did you realize this?

Vic: A few months ago. It was right after Natalie took our son and went to visit her mother for two weeks. . . . I didn't miss her at all.

M.L.: And this was different from the way you felt when you married Natalie?

Vic: Well, I'm sure I must have loved her very much then. If you want to know the truth, I married Natalie mostly because I felt a lot of obligation to do so. Not that she was pregnant or anything like that. It's just that I thought I didn't have much choice.

As the couple traced out the background of their story, it developed that Natalie had been married before. Victor, a bachelor, had been a close friend of her first husband. When the man began "acting strangely," as Natalie put it, Victor spent a good deal of time with the couple trying to cheer up his friend and help Natalie cope. He was not particularly successful in either effort—the husband grew more difficult, and Natalie more distressed and bewildered. As the weeks passed Vic and Natalie became increasingly involved with other emotionally. One night—the couple both agreed on this—she seduced him. They continued their sexual relationship until Victor's company sent him on a two-year assignment to the Middle East. While he was overseas Natalie got a divorce.

Vic: She kept writing to me all that time. She talked about us getting married when I came back home. It seemed as if she *expected* me to marry her, although I had never said anything about that, certainly never promised her anything.

M.L.: What was your reaction to the idea?

Vic: Well, I was afraid that somehow I was responsible for their breakup. I felt guilty, I guess. And Natalie kept saying how much she needed me, how happy she had been when we were together. I suppose I thought I ought to marry her. After all, I couldn't just run out on her, could I?

Shortly after Victor came back from the Middle East he and Natalie were married. A year later their child was born. According to both of them, they were quite happy. Then Vic had his change of heart.

Vic: It's just that I don't feel about her the way I did . . . the way I should.

Natalie (exasperated): I don't understand you at all. You don't act a bit different now from the way you did then. *(Turning to therapist.)* He *says* he doesn't love me, you'd never know it from the way he acts. Only six months ago he insisted we buy a new home. He just finished putting in the lawn. He still likes to make love to me, and our sex life is very good. He compliments my cooking. And he is always telling me I'm pretty. . . . Then he says he doesn't love me. . . . It doesn't add up.

Vic (helplessly): That's all true, including the love part. I'm just not in love with you any more.

Poor Natalie. She has had two husbands whose actions "didn't make sense" to her. She thought she was a good wife and a good lover to both of them, but both eventually behaved in "crazy" ways. "Maybe," Natalie began to think, "something is 'crazy' about me!" The counseling sessions continued.

M.L.: Vic, do you like the idea of being married?

Vic: Yes. I think I am a family man—a homebody, you know.

M.L.: Do you think you would be happier married to someone else?

Vic: There isn't anyone else, if that's what you're driving at. But I don't expect to stay single for long. I like sharing my life with a woman.

Natalie (interrupting): Then if you aren't interested in another woman, and you do want to be married, why not stay with *me?*

Vic (shaking his head): I can't explain it any better than I already have.

M.L.: Vic, do you think Natalie loves you?

Vic: Yes, I'd say so. But it's not fair for her to be married to a man who doesn't love her. She should be free to find someone who does.

Natalie: Divorcing me, that's your idea of fair?

As part of their marital therapy, both Victor and Natalie answered the Love Scale questions. Their scores were strikingly different. Victor rated highest in the Unselfish and next highest in the Best Friend categories. Natalie clearly was a Possessive, but with a substantial amount of the Romantic mixed in with that. Not unexpectedly, then, divorcing Natalie—leaving her free to pursue what Victor thought would be her own best interests—*was* his idea of being fair. Further counseling sessions disclosed that Victor had developed and internalized his concept of loving behavior as the only child of a widowed mother. He had learned to be one who gives. The girls he had dated were usually as emotionally troubled and needy as his mother was. Yet at the same time, Victor admitted to the counselor, he had envied other couples he described as "romantic." At some unconscious level Victor wanted to love and be loved in that way too, rather than always feeling he had to give of himself. But when he failed—or was reluctant—to live up to his Unselfish concepts of loving behavior he felt guilty.

For Victor, the stress of loving Natalie came not so much from trying to adapt to her Possessive and Romantic style of loving as, paradoxically, from his secret feeling that her definition of love was the "right" one. Nor did Natalie help to disabuse him of this idea. Had she not been miserable when she was away from him those two weeks? And had he not rather enjoyed being by himself? When Natalie accusingly implied that if Victor did not miss her, then he did not love her, Victor came to doubt his own definition of love even more. When Victor tried to analyze his situation the solution seemed clear: Having married Natalie in the first place because he did not want to disappoint her, he now felt he should remove himself from her life for the same reason. Unselfish lovers, you will recall, typically believe that love is ended when they no longer can fulfill a partner's emotional needs. Victor could not accept the idea that his way of loving was as valid as Natalie's—and perhaps as necessary to her. Instead, it seemed to him that she deserved a "better" kind of love than he could offer.

With the help of counseling, Victor and Natalie gradually came to understand the way in which their different styles of love had created the impasse between them. And by accepting the fact that no single style is necessarily "right" or "wrong," they were also able to accept each other's way of showing love. Although neither partner could make basic changes in their approach to loving and being loved, in time they were able to adjust to each other's styles well enough so their marriage could survive.

Recent studies of the rising divorce rate in America have tried to determine just what specific types of conflict are concealed by those nebulous no-fault grounds of "irremediable breakdown" and "irreconcilable differences." It is all very well to cite statistics that list such causes of divorce as poor communication, problems with children and money, sexual incompatibility, emotional abuse, and so on. But therapists know that these labels are merely the surface evidence of an underlying and unidentified disharmony. One can only wonder how many of these "causes" might well be subsumed under the single category of "mismatched love-style combinations."

When mismatches have reached the "I don't love you anymore" stage it is difficult even for a counselor or therapist to help. This is particularly true if a therapist falls into the trap of identifying one partner's love style as "better" and tries to help the other accept it; or, still more unfortunate, if a therapist unwittingly defines "true love" on the basis of his or her personal concept of loving, and tries to influence a couple to accept *that* as the ideal.

The lesson is clear: every couple needs to define—and then continually redefine—their unique pattern of loving. This is the cement that holds two people together. If mismatched partners are empathetic and flexible they can learn to accommodate love-style conflicts between them. But if a couple can become aware of the dynamics between their styles of loving *before* they establish a long-term partnership, it will be far more successful.

9
TOWARD MORE
EFFECTIVE LOVING

> The supreme happiness of life is the conviction
> that we are loved . . . loved for ourselves, or . . .
> in spite of ourselves.
>
> —Victor Hugo, *Les Misérables*

Marital therapist Carlfred Broderick often tells his clients
of an incident that occurred in the early days of his own
marriage. Having come down with the flu, Broderick took
to his bed and waited to be cared for by his bride. Specifically, he waited for her to bring him large glasses of
orange juice—something that his mother had always done
whenever he had been sick as a child. Now, though Broderick's wife paid attention to his needs in every other way,
no juice was forthcoming. Eventually the therapist said,
with what he thought was great tact, "Honey, I didn't
realize there wasn't any orange juice in the house." Taking
the hint, his wife brought him one small glass of juice.
When hours passed without a refill, Broderick asked for
more. Another small glassful appeared.

The same sequence of events continued for two more
days until finally the therapist's wife said with some an-
noyance, "What *is* this with you and orange juice? Even
when I get some for you it doesn't seem to satisfy you!"
Having grown up believing that, no matter what ails a
person, one gets better in direct proportion to the amount
of orange juice one is given, Broderick could not understand his wife's seeming lack of concern for his recovery.
"I was so hurt," he recalls, "that if I hadn't felt so weak
I would have left the house."

Later, when he was able to analyze the incident objectively, the therapist realized that he identified being given
endless glasses of orange juice with being loved. But he
had never made this clear to his wife. So far as she was

concerned, juice was juice and love was something one demonstrated by making sure that the patient followed doctor's orders.[1]

It has been said that the most important thing in life is to love someone, the second most important is to have someone love you, and the third most important is for the first two to happen at the same time. To these we would add a fourth most important condition: that each partner understands what makes the other feel truly loved. Unless we know that, most of what we do or say to show our love is likely to be misread.

A good example of ineffective loving behavior (oddly enough it also involves orange juice) occurred when the husband of a couple in counseling protested his wife's complaint that he seldom did anything to show he still loved her:

Husband: Don't I get up every morning before you do in order to squeeze fresh orange juice for your breakfast?
Wife: Yes, but that's just a habit you got into, and you don't know how to stop. I'm sure you hate doing it. Remember, I never *asked* for such a favor.
Husband: You've got it all wrong. I do that because it's one of the ways I can show you that I love you.
Wife (surprised): Really? Is that what it means to you? It wouldn't to me, I'd just hate doing that every morning. . . . I never thought of it as a loving gesture. . . . I thought you were trying to make me feel obligated in some way.

Despite the paucity of research into the parameters of love, most studies that have been done point to the same single factor as the critical one when a person decides whether or not he or she is in love. Though it is called by different names—caring, consideration, thoughtfulness—it comes down to this: the belief that we understand the emotional motivation behind a partner's words and actions, and that he or she similarly understands ours. "The voice of the intellect is small but it will have a hearing," said Freud. And it does seem that love may depend less on emotional or physiological reactions than we have previously assumed, and more on intellectual awareness—"My partner and I *know* what love means to each of us."

To put it another way, it is the ability to be empathetic

that is the essential ingredient. Empathy is not the same as sympathy; it functions on a different level. When we are sympathetic we are able to *feel*, with some accuracy, the same emotion another person is experiencing. But when we are empathetic we are able to *understand intellectually* not only what the other person is feeling but also the reasons for his or her emotional reaction. Sympathy is sameness of feeling; empathy is mental awareness of that feeling.

For example, a mother sees her child cry and hit out when another youngster takes away a toy. If the mother experiences only the same surge of anger and resentment the child feels at that moment, she is being sympathetic. But if she mentally comprehends the child's response she is being empathetic. She may have her own set of emotional reactions to the incident, ranging from pity to anger to protectiveness; or she may have no particular emotional response at all to the situation. The point is that she understands and identifies with the child's distress.

Ignorance of the differences that exist among love styles is a fundamental barrier to empathy. To understand another person's approach to love even though you do not share it; to recognize and accept the love that lies behind another's action even though you yourself may express love in quite a different way—those are the skills at the heart of effective loving.

LEARNING TO LOVE MORE EFFECTIVELY

The first step toward more effective loving is to acquire as much insight as possible into your own and your partner's love styles. This does not mean simply establishing via the Love Scale Questionnaire how each of you defines love. Since love is a subjective experience, terminology alone will not tell you much more about each other's approach to it than defining salt as sodium chloride will tell you how it tastes. Real insight into your mutual ideas about loving behavior can come only with a frank exploration of what words, actions, and attitudes make each of you feel truly loved.

It is surprising how many men and women draw a blank when they are asked to be specific about love. Most people are not clearly aware of their needs or wishes, much less able to put them into words. Some believe that a lover or spouse ought to be able to sense such things without having to be told about them: "If you loved me you'd know what I need." But love does not automatically make one a skilled mind reader. Most of the time lovers do have to guess at each other's inner needs. As a result, they are likely to offer the kinds of responses they themselves would like to get. These responses are often far off the target.

Here is an example from the case file of a recent counseling client, a man whose Logical love style prevented him from sensing his wife's emotional need:

"My wife's eighty-five-year-old mother died not long ago after a long illness. She had lived in Texas and the funeral services were to be held there, fifteen hundred miles from our home. I didn't see any reason for me to take a week off from work to accompany my wife, and she didn't even suggest that I go with her. After all, my mother-in-law had lived a long and full life, and her death did not come as a sudden shock. My wife seemed to take the news quite camly.

"So I did what I thought would be most helpful. I made her plane reservations, drove her to the airport, took care of arranging for a sitter to be in the house when our children got home from school. I thought I was doing everything I could to show my love and concern. And my wife never gave a sign that she wanted anything more from me, that I was somehow 'failing' her.

"Yet when she came back from Texas she was furious with me. 'How could you let me go through that alone?' she shouted. 'If you loved me you woud have gone with me! But you never even had the decency to offer!' I was amazed. I mean, if she had wanted me to go with her, all she had to do was tell me."

If you have a problem telling a partner what would make you feel loved, you are not alone. The difficulty is twofold. First, many men and women seem to find it embarrassing to discuss the subject. The embarrassment stems from at least two sources. One is the fact that talking about feelings is perhaps the most self-revealing kind of communication. It opens us up to another person, makes us feel emotionally naked. And in this vulnerable position we are left, so it seems, completely unguarded against criticism or rejection.

The other source of embarrassment is that what we need from a partner often seems a bit silly, even to ourselves. The words or actions we long for as evidence of love may well be—as in the case of the therapist and the orange juice—a throwback to something our parents did for us or said to us when we were children. But we may feel that to admit that kind of an "infantile" reaction is a sign of weakness. The truth is just the opposite. To be able to share such an intimate revelation with a partner—and to feel emotionally safe in doing so—is a sign not of weakness but of mutual trust. It is proof of love's strength when lovers can talk freely about what makes them feel loved.

The second reason many of us find it difficult to express our emotional needs is that we often do not know exactly what we are looking for. We have not really clarified our attitudes about the kind of behavior we define as loving. A good way to start dealing with this obstacle is to ask yourself these questions:

Do I know what my expectations of love are and how realistic they may be? Each of us, consciously or not, holds a set of assumptions about how we are supposed to feel and act when we are in love, and how a lover should feel and act toward us. These expectations are the product of all our experiences—the books we read, the films we see, the way we were raised, how our parents behaved toward each other, the romantic daydreams we have, the goals we seek, the values we cherish. When these expectations are uncritically internalized, they can lead to fixed but unrealistic ideas about loving behavior: "Anyone who loves me will always be considerate of my smallest wish." . . . "If my wife loves me she will be willing to have sex any time I want to." . . . "If my husband loves me he will never go anywhere without me." Even when a couple's love styles mesh well, one or the other partner's expectations may be too grandoise, too rigid, or impossible to be fulfilled.

Are my expectations so open-ended that I cannot feel truly loved no matter what my partner says or does? Some people cannot permit themselves the sense of emotional contentment, of being loved, because they always have another expectation waiting to be filled. They are never quite satisfied with a partner's attempts to show love. If the longed-for gift is given, the card does not have the right sentiment. If the desired action is forthcoming, it isn't timed well or does not measure up to some hard-to-define or constantly elevated standard. "Whatever I do for my wife doesn't seem to be enough," one discouraged husband complained. "It's as if I were a high jumper in a competition that I'm not allowed to win. I clear the bar and expect some kind of acknowledgment for what I have done. Instead, she raises the bar a notch higher."

Am I sufficiently in touch with my expectations about love so that I can tell whether or not they are being met? The quickest way to get in touch is to know what does *not* make you feel loved, to be aware of those occasions when you feel *un*loved. Such information can provide accurate clues to whether you expected some sign of loving behavior that you did not get, or whether you received a response you did not anticipate or did not interpret as loving. As psychiatrist Erik Erikson observes in his book, *Identity, Youth and Crisis,* people know what they do *not* want long before they know what they want. Erikson calls this "negative identity." This is an identity based on rejection of one's earlier roles, rejection of one's identification with parents. The teen-ager who rebels against family traditions for the sake of rebelling, the student who drops out of college to "find himself," the stockbroker who quits his job to sail a charter boat in the Caribbean—these are all typical examples of the syndrome.

Such acts of rejection are dictated by a strong motivation to find one's unique niche in life—even if that niche leaves much to be desired. So our first ideas about who we are and what we want are based on who we are *not* and what we do *not* want. Erikson suggests that awareness of our dislikes may be a necessary development step toward awareness of our preferences. For many of us, then, efforts to share with a partner how we want to be loved may find their earliest expression in negatives: "Love isn't just wine and roses." . . . "If there's no good sex, there's no real love."

While negative feelings may not lead directly to awareness of what we want, indirectly they point to what is missing. When you recognize negative feelings, ask yourself, "What did I expect just then?" Following this procedure would have saved one couple we know from disappointment. The husband, an advertising executive, had to travel to Florida for a crucial interview with a prospective client. Ordinarily he made such trips without his wife. On this occasion he surprised her by asking if she wanted to go with him. The woman hesitated briefly, then said: "Well . . . if you'd like me to go along I guess I could."

"Don't you think you would enjoy it?" the man asked.

"Oh yes," she replied. "But wouldn't it complicate things for you, interfere with your work? The trip doesn't matter that much to me one way or the other, really. There are lots of things I can do here while you're away."

"I see," the man said. Then, after a moment's silence, "Very well, if that's how you feel I'll go by myself."

Unbeknownst to each other, both partners felt severely disappointed and unloved. The husband had very much wanted his wife to accompany him. He felt a need for her emotional support. But her seeming reluctance to leave home convinced him that she did not care enough about him to meet that need. For her part, the wife was not sure her husband sincerely meant his invitation. Although she wanted to go with him, she felt she should give him a face-saving excuse to travel alone. "If he really wanted me along"—i.e., if he really loved me—"he would have insisted," she thought. In short, each assumed the other's behavior was unloving. Two people who wanted desperately to show their love for each other—but who could not communicate their expectations and feelings for fear of rejection—ended by believing each had *been* rejected.

To overcome the misunderstanding caused by such faulty communication we need to develop patience and sensitivity to what a partner says or may be trying to say. If it seems advisable, each person ought to explain clearly what feelings are at stake, so that each has a realistic idea of what the other expects in terms of loving behavior. It is not fair to assume that our partner should somehow magically "know" what we want. "If we want to be loved, we must disclose ourselves," said the late Dr. Sidney Jourard, a psychologist and human relations counselor, "and if we want to love someone, he must permit us to know him." Mutual self-disclosure is a key step toward more effective loving. Most of us never take it. Either we remain unaware of its importance or we fear the emotional vulnerability it creates.

Some couples are lucky enough to be on the same communication wave length. Others must work hard to understand what each is trying to say. And some never manage to do that. Yet each partner continues to expect that he or she always ought to understand—or be understood by—the other. "I don't know what my wife is trying to tell me," a man says. "She talks in such a vague way that our conversation never stays on one topic, never heads in a single direction. And then she acts hurt if I can't figure out what's bothering her." Alone with the counselor, the woman defends herself: "I'm afraid of what might happen if I said what I really feel. To say I don't feel loved . . . that would hurt my husband."

Probably the most infuriating kind of inaccurate communication above love is what therapists call a "double bind." That occurs when a person is given two conflicting messages that apply to the same situation—and therefore is wrong no matter which message he or she acts upon. A classic double-bind involvement was presented by a couple who consulted a sex therapist to find out why the frequency of their love-making had dropped almost to zero. Their problem began, the woman explained, when her husband accused her of not really loving him because she never took the sexual initiative. But when, after his remarks, she did on occasion take the initiative, the man seemed displeased. Though he had asked her to behave that way, he was upset when she did.

Obviously the husband was ambivalent about wanting his wife to be sexually assertive. But though *he* may have been unaware that he was sending a paradoxical message, his wife was still faced with a Catch-22 situation. To show her love, she had to try to guess what her husband wanted her to do at any given time even though he did not know that himself. Whatever she did—take the sexual initiative or not—was almost guaranteed to be wrong. Damned if she did and damned if she didn't, the harder the woman tried to resolve her dilemma the more maddening the situation grew. When all one's well-intentioned responses accomplish nothing save continue to arouse the other person's displeasure, one eventually thinks, "Why bother?" and stops trying. Which, of course, is what this woman instinctively, self-protectively, did. The result: both partners felt frustrated, unhappy, and unloved.

A second step toward more effective loving is to accept the fact that, though two people may have different or even conflicting love styles, neither has a monopoly on propriety or truth. We have said this before but it is important enough to warrant repetition. Too many men and women talk about the "right" way to love. A Logical lover may find it hard to think of a Game Player in anything but negative terms, for instance. Yet there is no one correct approach to loving. It is self-defeating to believe otherwise. For if one feels his or her style is the only right style, it is all too easy to feel that the other styles are not really "love" at all. Almost every marital therapist has witnessed one variation or another of this typical scenario:

Hilary has decided that she must leave Dan, her husband of fifteen years. She does not love him anymore. Even though he is a good man, she says, he has "killed" her love. The couple have come to the therapist's office at Dan's request, for he wants to save his marriage. He has listened carefully to the charges that Hilary levels against him.

Dan: I don't understand what you want, I guess. Heaven knows I've done everything I can to try to please you.
Hilary (compassionate but inflexible): I know you have, but it's no use, Dan. You can never bring back the feelings in me that have died.
Dan: Just because I took you for granted sometimes? Just because I was too tired to be "romantic" when I was working twelve hours a day to earn our living? Surely that can't erase all our years together. Doesn't all that we've been through together mean anything to you?
Hilary: Of course it does. But I want something you evidently can't give me.
Therapist: What is that, Hilary?
Hilary: I'm not even sure myself. But I know that I've been greatly disappointed in my dreams of love with Dan. There's no romance, no excitement with him at all. He doesn't seem to know the real meaning of love.
Dan: You're being completely illogical, Hilary, as usual. Love isn't always supposed to be excitement and romance.
Hilary: No? You tell me what it's supposed to be—as if I can't guess.

Dan: Love is doing what you have to do. It's the daily routine of work, kids, sharing, being partners in life. The trouble with you, Hilary, is that your ideas of love are dead wrong.

Therapist: Hilary has a right to her concept of what love is, Dan, just as you have a right to yours. It's unfortunate that your ideas about loving are so far apart. But for either of you to attack the other on that basis is bound to defeat any hope you have of improving matters between you. No definition of love is "wrong." It is only different.

Hilary and Dan illustrate a fundamental principle involved in falling *out* of love (as well as *into* it): Hilary "knew" she no longer loved Dan because of her changed *feelings* toward him. Dan's realization that his wife no longer loved him was based on her *behavior*—what she did or didn't do. Ultimately Dan said that he did understand how his actions might have caused Hilary's feelings for him to shut down. He even tried to make significant changes in his behavior. But so far as Hilary was concerned they came too late. Moreover, she suggested that their inability to recognize each other's right to their individual views of love meant that, even if their surface relationship worked better, they would still be miles apart in understanding. The therapist realized that Hilary was probably correct in her assessment. The underlying problem between Dan the Logical and Hilary the Romantic lover was each one's judgmental attitude toward the other's love style. Instead of communicating about love in a positive way, the couple were caught up in negative approaches. Instead of saying, "This is what you can do to make me feel loved," they had gotten trapped in the habit of saying, "This is what you do that makes me feel unloved."

The third step toward effective loving is to be able and willing to make changes in the way you characteristically demonstrate your love, changes designed to mesh your behavior with your partner's love style. "If only he were more affectionate," sighs the Romantic wife. "If only she would understand that when I need to be alone sometimes it doesn't mean I'm rejecting her," says the Best Friend lover of a Possessive sweetheart.

The human capacity for change is enormous. Most of us are able to adapt our behavior to the standards or wishes of others so that we can get along with them better. We do this with bosses, teachers, friends, even whole environments. Yet at the same time there is a strong tendency to resist change, especially in the framework of our most intimate relationships. Indeed, the prospect of change can be so distressing that many people struggle against it vehemently. Some take an unyielding stance: "I am what I am and how I am, take me or leave me." Others play on a partner's guilt: "If you really cared for me you'd love me just the same." Still others retreat to the defensive: "I simply can't help it, I can't change." And perhaps they really believe they cannot; it is easier than facing up to the fact that they do not *want* to change.

Why do so many men and women so stubbornly resist making changes that would help a partner to feel better loved? There are four basic reasons:

• If one needs to be the controlling partner in a relationship, making a change to accommodate the other person's needs may be seen as a loss of power and dominance. There are some people whose drive to be in charge outweighs their desire for a mutually rewarding love relationship. Accommodation is seen as "losing," since it requires an acknowledgment that one's partner may have a valid even if opposing view of "proper" loving behavior.

• Change is a troublesome activity, and some men and women are too lazy to try. Most of us are creatures of habit, and making changes means that we will have to think about our new behavior, be aware of our actions. This takes effort, energy, and will power. It is easier to do things the old way, even if we know that the old way may not be the better way.

• Some people fear what may happen if they change. To embark on a new and different course is a challenge they find too dangerous—or at least too emotionally uncomfortable—to meet. Change makes them anxious. Why risk rocking the boat? they wonder. A Best Friend/Logical lover told us:

"I know my husband would like it if I showed him more affection and told him more often that I love him. But I just can't bring myself to do it. I've never found it easy to be demonstrative; it actually makes me uncomfortable. We've gotten along okay the way I am all these years, so why should I suddenly have to change my whole personality?"

• Finally, some people are too self-centered to change. They think the *other* person should change. They view change as an admission of error. It seems to them to imply that whatever they have been doing is faulty, ineffective, wrong. Frequently such a person's refusal to change is passive in nature. Rather than flatly telling the other person that he or she must do the changing, the self-centered partner simply makes no move to act differently no matter how the request is made:

"No, I don't argue about it," a young husband says, "I just know that my wife has everything she needs to make any woman feel loved. If she doesn't, that's *her* problem. She says I'm away too much, or preoccupied with business when I am home. But she will just have to learn that I am a very busy man. There's nothing I can do to change that. So I simply ignore her complaints."

Change in the context of caring behavior does not mean abandoning your own love style and cultivating a different one. That would be virtually impossible even if you wanted to do so. It does mean cultivating some flexibility—making an effort to please or to reassure a partner by responding in ways that he or she interprets as signs of love even though you may not construe them as such yourself.

In recent years behavior modification has become a popular and effective technique for overcoming resistances and encouraging change. Essentially, one person "modifies" the other's behavior by giving something in exchange for what he or she gets. A common example might be that of a woman who agrees to make her husband's favorite dessert twice a week in return for his taking care of getting her car washed and serviced regularly. To some people this quid pro quo process seems artificial and manipulative. However, it is useful in achieving simple or highly specific behavioral changes. And it is no doubt more amiable to be manipulated by rewards than by criticisms.

When the desired change is more subtle and complex, tit-for-tat bargaining is not likely to be as productive as *joint negotiation* between partners. Often there is no way, in such situations, of making a quid pro quo arrangement that both persons can perceive as "even." Something more —understanding, empathy, a willingness to give more or ask less—is required. Negotiation, therefore, depends for its success on the degree of trust and respect two people have for each other, and on the extent to which they genuinely want to improve their relationship.

There are four important steps involved in helping a partner to change through negotiation:

1. Both persons need to talk honestly and calmly about the behavior in question and about the changes involved —why one partner seeks the change, why the other objects, what goals the change would help to achieve. If you are not sure what would make your partner feel loved, *ask.* Verbal "distractors" such as criticism, nagging, or angry outbursts do not produce constructive results.

2. The person who is asking a partner to change must be highly specific about just what he or she wants the other person to do or to stop doing. For example, suppose Mary resents the fact that John brings home a briefcase full of business papers every evening and spend the hours between dinner and bedtime working on them. Instead of attacking John by saying something like, "If you loved me you would pay more atttention to me when you're home!" Mary might say:

"John, I would appreciate it if you could spend a little more time with me in the evenings. I'd enjoy talking to you."

Note that Mary does not dwell on what John does that annoys her, nor does she berate him for doing it.

3. Mary now spells out the advantages that would accrue to John as a result of changing his behavior:

"If you spent more time with me after dinner, we'd be able to share more of our experiences, and I'd feel closer to you than I do."

4. Now it is John's turn to respond to Mary's request. He may agree:

"I didn't realize I was bringing that much work home every night. You're right, Mary, we should have more time for each other."

Or he may ask for a postponement of the discussion so he can have more time to think about what Mary said:

"I really wasn't aware you felt lonely. I'd like to think about this situation for a while, maybe keep track of just how much work I do bring home and then let's talk about it again."

John may suggest a compromise:

"I didn't mean to ignore you, Mary. But you have no idea of how much I have to do at the office. The only time I have to catch up on paperwork is in the evenings. But suppose I bring home only as much as I can do in an hour. Then we'll have the rest of the time for ourselves. How's that?"

Or John may flatly disagree with Mary's suggestion:

"We talk during dinner, and that seems to cover pretty much everything we have to say to each other. Besides, bringing work home is a good way to impress my boss."

In three out of these four scenarios the negotiation process is left unfinished. If one partner asks for more time to consider the situation, both should try to establish a specific time when they can talk about it again. An offer to compromise should be accepted and encouraged—but not necessarily viewed as a final step. Once a person has made even a small move in the direction of change, he or she often finds that other or larger changes in that same direction become easier to make. Even total disagreement need not be viewed as a permanent rebuff. Mary may have asked for too great a change. Perhaps John can suggest a different way of arriving at the same goal.

When we talk about helping a partner to change it is important to remember that we are talking about behavioral change only. It is extremely difficult, if not impossible, to directly change another person's way of thinking or feeling. We may get someone to agree to spend more time with us, or to control jealous outbursts, but that does not mean he or she will necessarily want to do that, or think it's a good idea, or be able to do so consistently.

Here are other suggestions for helping you and your partner adapt to each other's love styles:
• Look back at the early days of your relationship and try to recall the things you said and did then to show your loving feelings. Perhaps you were more generous with compliments, exchanged small gifts, sent each other sentimental notes. During courtship and in the first years of marriage

we are most highly attuned to the needs and wishes of our partner. We spend a good deal of time and energy trying to detect and understand what the one we love wants. We convince him or her of *our* love by saying and doing what we have come to know the other person considers to be signs of love. But slowly the newness fades, and the day-to-day problems of earning a living and raising a family demand our attention. Preoccupation and fatigue often block out loving thoughts and actions. If only we could be as attentive, warm, and kind to those we claim to love as we are to casual acquaintances and business colleagues!

People do change and what may have worked in the past to make your relationship a loving one may have lost some of its effectiveness now. Experiment through trial and error to find out what actions on your part provoke the desired responses.

• Your partner can give you valuable clues about what would make him or her feel loved by how he or she shows love to you. One man we know took weeks to plan an elaborate birthday celebration for his wife, complete with surprise party, even though he knew she never made much of a fuss about birthdays. It should have been a clear message to her that he hoped she would respond in kind on his birthday. Wisely, she did. Though the woman secretly felt it was a childish thing to do, she arranged a lavish celebration. She knew it would make her husband feel that he was truly loved.

• Think of change not as giving something up but as a way of getting emotional rewards. "I do a lot of things for my wife that I wouldn't care if she never did for me," one man told us. "But when I do she is so appreciative that I get tremendous pleasure just out of having done them. She knows that I love her. And so she does things for me that *I* need, to feel loved. We have truly learned to make the effort to love each other the way the other wants to be loved." Some couples reward each other this way intuitively. Others help to bring about behavior changes by using the technique of positive reinforcement as a deliberate tool. A Romantic woman, distressed by her husband's chronic thoughtlessness, waited patiently until the opportunity arose for her to praise him for some small considerate act. "When he finally remembered to bring home a book I had asked for *four* times," she said, "I thanked him as if it were a diamond necklace. He looked at me oddly, but I could see he was pleased. I did the same thing on several subsequent occasions, and gradually my husband began to want to be attentive toward me because he enjoyed being appreciated so much."

• Consider professional counseling as a way to help you develop more insight into your and your partner's love styles, and to help you mediate any changes that will enable them to mesh more effectively. "One of my clients was a highly Romantic woman who felt she was no longer in love with her partner because sexual excitement had declined," a therapist recalls. "She felt the only solution was to leave him. But I was able to point out to her that sexual excitement declines in virtually every long-term relationship, and that it did not necessarily mean she did not love the man any longer, or that he didn't love her. I also helped her to realize that sexual pleasure was still possible, and to recognize other values in her marriage which she had not recognized or had overlooked." A Possessive wife who was jealous of her husband's demanding job was helped by a counselor to recognize the pressures the man faced from his superiors, and to realize that part of her jealousy of the man's involvement in his work was due to discontent with her own emotional dependency. "When love styles conflict," one therapist said, "partners often see only one way out—separation. It's my job to show them alternatives. Perhaps to learn new ways of responding. Perhaps to make some changes in their definitions of love."

Paradoxically, change may be the one area of human relationships in which the Golden Rule might better read, "Do *not* necessarily do unto others as you would have others do unto you." Instead of this scenario—

"I love you."
"You do?"
"Of course, can't you tell?"
"How would I know it from the way you act?"

—a knowledge of love styles plus the capacity to change behavior might produce this:

"I love you."
"I know."
"How?"
"By the things you do and say."

But change cannot be forced. The humanistic therapist Fritz Perls used to say: "You can't push the river. . . ." Trying to force changes in a partner's loving behavior is something like trying to push the river. One can, however, move a river in other ways: by diverting it into new channels, by damming it in one place and deeping it in another. So can we encourage change in our partners and in ourselves. "I cannot change the way you love me," a man said to his wife recently, "I can only influence you to change." That influence, when wisely applied, can be the catalyst for growth in mutual understanding and love.

A NOTE ON SOURCES

Almost all of the anecdotal material used to illustrate various aspects of love styles stems from personal interviews, personal communications, and case histories from Marcia Lasswell's counseling experience. Additional material and insights were derived from many of the "What I believe love is . . ." statements written by respondents before they took the Love Scale Questionnaire. The following give more specific sources of data not completely identified in the text.

PREFACE

1. The incident of the professor's questionnaire is recounted by Dr. Ellen Berscheid and Jack Fei, "Romantic Love and Sexual Jealousy," in *Jealousy*, Gordon Clanton and Lynn Smith, eds. (New York: Prentice-Hall, 1977).

CHAPTER 1

1. Reflects statistical findings of various national polls.
2. The rarity of research on love is mentioned by many family sociologists, especially William M. Kephart, "Some Correlates of Romantic Love," *Journal of Marriage and the Family*, Vol. 29 (1967) No. 3.
3. Carol Tavris and Toby Epstein Jayaratne, "How Happy Is Your Marriage?" *Redbook* (June 1976).
4. Dr. Aron Krich and Sam Blum, "Marriage and the Mystique of Romance," *Redbook* (November 1970).
5. John Alan Lee, *The Colours of Love* (Toronto: New Press, 1975).

CHAPTER 2

1. That young people fall "in love" several times before the age of eighteen is indicated by the research findings of Dr. Carlfred Broderick.

2. Erich Fromm, *The Art of Loving* (New York: Harper, 1956).

3. Refers to studies by Dr. Paul MacLean, of the National Institute of Mental Health's Laboratory of Brain Evolution and Behavior, as reported in his *A Triune Concept of Brain and Behavior* (Toronto: University of Toronto Press, 1973).

4. Roderic Gorney, *The Human Agenda* (New York: Simon & Schuster, 1968, 1972).

5. Stephen P. Hersh and Karen Levin, "How Love Begins Between Parent and Child," *Children Today* (March–April 1978).

6. Dr. Brazelton's comments are from his "How Babies Learn About Love," *Redbook* (July 1977).

7. Harlow's experiments were first reported in his article, "The Nature of Love," *American Psychologist,* Vol. 13 (1958).

8. Brazelton, op. cit.

9. The relationship between self-esteem and the capacity to love is explored at length by Dr. Honor Whitney in her handbook, "How Many Times Do I Have to Tell You . . ." (1976).

10. The result of a study conducted by psychologist Dr. Robert M. Gordon for a doctoral thesis.

11. The effect of birth order on attitudes toward love is reported by Dr. Lucille K. Forer, *Birth Order and Life Roles* (Springfield, Ill.: Charles C. Thomas, 1969).

12. The observations are by Dr. Carlfred Broderick and Dr. George P. Rowe, "A Scale of Pre-Adolescent Heterosexual Development," *Journal of Marriage and the Family,* Vol. 30 (1968) No. 1.

CHAPTER 3

1. Theodor Reik, *The Need to Be Loved* (New York: Bantam, 1964).

2. An exhaustive source of data on cultural attitudes toward love is Dr. Bernard I. Murstein, *Love, Sex and Marriage Through the Ages* (New York: Springer, 1974).

3. The Dijon anecdote is mentioned by Nina Epton in *Love and the French* (London: Cassell, 1959).

4. The incident of the baseball player and his admirer

was reported by Milton Richman in the Los Angeles *Times,* March 18, 1978.

5. Dr. Roberts' research was reported by Harry Nelson in the Los Angeles *Times,* March 31, 1974.
6. For a fuller discussion of pheromones, see Ron Davids, "Talking Without Words," *Science Digest* (February 1973).
7. Reported by A. M. Katz and R. Hill, "Residential Propinquity and Marital Selection," *Marriage and Family Living,* Vol. 20 (1958).
8. Dr. Armacost's quote is from a personal communication.
9. Theodor Reik, *A Psychologist Looks at Love* (New York: Farrar & Rinehart, 1944).
10. Robert F. Winch, *Mate Selection* (New York: Harper, 1958).
11. The exchange theory of love was formulated by Dr. Bernard I. Murstein. See his *Who Will Marry Whom?* (New York: Springer, 1976).

CHAPTER 4

1. "A Taxonomy of Love," an unpublished paper by Dr. Bernard I. Murstein.
2. Reported by S. Valins, "Cognitive Effects of False Heart-Rate Feedback," *Journal of Personality and Social Psychology,* Vol. 4 (1966).
3. Ira Reiss, "Toward a Sociology of the Heterosexual Love Relationship," *Marriage and Family Living,* Vol. 22 (1960).
4. The first report of the Lasswell-Hatkoff research on love styles was made by Dr. Thomas E. Lasswell and Marcia Lasswell at the November 1975 Annual Meeting of the American Association of Marital and Family Therapy, and published as "I Love You but I'm Not in Love with You," *Journal of Marriage and Family Counseling,* Vol. 2 (1976).

CHAPTER 5

1. The incident recounted by Dr. Robert Seidenberg appears in his essay, "Fidelity and Jealousy," *Psychoanalytic Review,* Vol. 54 (1967).
2. Stanton Peele with A. Brodsky, *Love and Addiction* (New York: Taplinger, 1975).
3. The comment from Zelda Fitzgerald was in a letter

to F. Scott Fitzgerald reprinted in *Love Letters,* an anthology chosen by Antonia Fraser (New York: Knopf, 1976, 1977).

4. The excerpt from Richard Steele was in a letter reprinted in *Love Letters of Great Men and Women,* C. H. Charles, ed. (London: Stanley Paul, 1924).

5. Anne Morrow Lindbergh's description of her first glimpse of Colonel Lindbergh is part of a diary entry published in *Bring Me a Unicorn,* a Helen and Kurt Wolff book (New York: Harcourt Brace Jovanovich, 1971, 1972).

6. Many of these observations are based on findings reported by Terry S. Hatkoff and Thomas E. Lasswell, "Male/Female Similarities and Differences in Conceptualizing Love," in *Love and Attraction,* Mark Cook, ed. (London: Pergamon, 1979).

7. William Kephart, op. cit.

CHAPTER 7

1. Tahitian love customs are described in A. Denis, *Taboo* (New York: Putnam, 1967).

2. Morton M. Hunt, *The Natural History of Love* (New York: Knopf, 1959).

3. Data on the relationship among sex, love, and song lyrics is reported in Melville L. Wilkinson, "Romantic Love and Sexual Expression," *The Family Coordinator,* Vol. 27 (1978).

4. Simone de Beauvoir is quoted in *People* (February 19, 1979).

5. John Alan Lee, op. cit.

6. Seidenberg, op. cit.

7. In a letter from Chopin to Delphine Potocka, *Love Letters,* Antonia Fraser, ed.

8. For additional insights, see Dr. Herbert S. Strean, "The Extramarital Affair," *Psychoanalytic Review,* Vol. 63 (1976).

9. Marvin Zuckerman, "The Sensation-Seeking Motive," in *Progress in Experimental Personality Research,* Vol. 7, B. Maher, ed. (New York: Academic Press, 1974).

CHAPTER 8

1. Liv Ullman, *Changing* (New York: Knopf, 1977).

2. The Kissingers' comments were reported in Trude B.

Feldman, "The Kissingers Talk About Their Marriage," *McCall's* (February 1976).

3. Original research on mismatches appears in "When Love Is Gone," an unpublished paper by Thomas E. Lasswell.

4. Sheilah Graham, *Beloved Infidel* (New York: Holt, 1958).

CHAPTER 9

1. Dr. Broderick's anecdote is recounted in his book *Couples: How to Confront Problems and Maintain Loving Relationships* (New York: Simon & Schuster, 1979).

BIBLIOGRAPHY

Bedier, Joseph. *The Romance of Tristan and Iseult*. Garden City, N.Y.: Doubleday, 1953.

Charles, C. H., ed. *Love Letters of Great Men and Women*. London: Stanley Paul, 1924.

Clanton, Gordon, and Smith, Lynn, eds. *Jealousy*. Englewood Cliffs, N.J.: Prentice-Hall, 1977.

Davenport, G. L. *Great Loves in Legend and Life*. New York: Franklin Watts, 1964.

de Rougement, Denis. *Love in the Western World*. New York: Harcourt, Brace, 1940.

————. *Love Declared*. New York: Pantheon, 1963.

Farber, Leslie. "On Jealousy," *Commentary* (October 1973).

Fraiberg, Selma. "The Origins of Human Bonds," *Commentary* (December 1967).

Fromm, Erich. *The Art of Loving*. New York: Harper, 1956.

Fromme, Allan. *The Ability to Love*. New York: Farrar, Straus, 1965.

Goode, William J. "The Theoretical Importance of Love," *American Sociological Review*, Vol. 24 (1959).

Hatkoff, Terry S. "Cultural and Demographic Differences in Persons' Cognitive Referents of Love." Unpublished doctoral dissertation, University of Southern California, 1978.

————. "Racial and Gender Differences in Persons' Cognitive Referents of Love." Unpublished paper presented at Pacific Sociological Association meetings, Spokane, Wash., 1978.

————, and Lasswell, Thomas E. "Love and Life Course Experiences." Unpublished paper presented at International Conference on Love and Attraction, 1977.

Hinkle, D. E., and Sporakowski, M. J. "Attitudes Toward

Love: A Re-examination," *Journal of Marriage and the Family,* Vol. 37 (1975).

Hunt, Morton. *The Natural History of Love.* New York: Knopf, 1959.

Lasswell, Marcia, and Lobsenz, Norman. *No-Fault Marriage.* Garden City, N.Y.: Doubleday, 1976.

Lasswell, Thomas E., and Lasswell, Marcia. "I Love You but I'm Not in Love with You," *Journal of Marriage and Family Counseling,* Vol. 2 (1976).

————, Hegy, Noreen, and Lasswell, Marcia. "Cognitive Referents of Love." Unpublished paper, 1974.

Lee, John Alan. *The Colours of Love.* Toronto: New Press, 1975.

Lobsenz, Norman. "What Do They See in Each Other?" *Woman's Day* (July 1974).

————. "How to Give and Get More Emotional Support," *Woman's Day* (September 20, 1977).

————. "Ten Questions Couples Ask Marriage Counselors Most," *Reader's Digest* (June 1976).

————. "Taming the Green-eyed Monster," *Redbook* (March 1975).

————, and Murstein, Bernard I. "Keeping Score," *Woman's Day* (September 1976).

Magoun, Alexander. *Love and Marriage.* New York: Harper, 1956.

Miller, H. L., and Siegel, P. S. *Loving: A Psychological Approach.* New York: John Wiley, 1972.

Murstein, Bernard I. "Stimulus-value-role: A Theory of Marital Choice," *Journal of Marriage and the Family,* Vol. 32 (1970).

————. *Theories of Attraction and Love.* New York: Springer, 1971.

————. *Love, Sex and Marriage Through the Ages.* New York: Springer, 1974.

————. *Who Will Marry Whom?* New York: Springer, 1976.

Ortega y Gasset. *On Love.* New York: New American Library, 1957.

Otto, H. A., ed. *Love Today: A New Exploration.* New York: Dell, 1972.

Ovid. *The Art of Love.* New York: Liveright, 1931.

Peele, Stanton, with Brodsky, A. *Love and Addiction.* New York: Taplinger, 1975.

Plutarch. *On Love, the Family and the Good Life.* New York: New American Library, 1957.

Reik, Theodor. *A Psychologist Looks at Love.* New York: Farrar & Rinehart, 1944.

————. *The Need to Be Loved.* New York: Bantam, 1964.

Rubin, Zick. *Liking and Loving.* New York: Holt, Rinehart & Winston, 1973.

————. "Measurements of Romantic Love," *Journal of Personality and Social Psychology,* Vol. 16 (1970).

Schlesinger, Arthur. "An Informal History of Love, U.S.A.," *Saturday Evening Post* (December 31, 1966).

Schneider, I., ed. *The World of Love.* New York: Braziller, 1964.

Stendhal (Marie Henri Beyle). *On Love.* New York: Boni & Liveright, 1927.

Udry, J. R. *The Social Context of Marriage.* Philadelphia: Lippincott, 1971.

Van Den Haag, Ernest. "Love or Marriage?" *Harper's* (May 1962).

Walster, Elaine, and Walster, G. William. *A New Look at Love.* Menlo Park, Cal.: Addison-Wesley, 1978.

Wilson, Glenn, and Nias, David. *The Mystery of Love.* New York: Quadrangle/New York Times, 1976.

Winch, Robert F. *Mate Selection: A Study of Complementary Needs.* New York: Harper, 1958.